Praise for
Orchestrating Transformation

Orchestrating Transformation is an exceptional read for CEOs in this age of frequent technological disruption. You'll get timeless tools, tactics, and frameworks to help you transform your business and adapt as artificial intelligence and digital technologies reshape your industry.

— **Kai-Fu Lee,** founder and CEO of Sinovation Ventures

The reason many digital transformation programs fail has little to do with ambition and technology. It is mainly about execution. Digital transformation, at scale, respects none of the traditional organizational boundaries that we have created. In **Orchestrating Transformation,** *the authors dig deep into the "How" of digital transformation and provide hard-won lessons from many companies' successes and failures. As we face perpetual cycles of increasingly complex digital change, this book is timely for both practitioners and business leaders who want to turn the odds of transformation in their favor.*

— **Didier Bonnet,** co-author, *Leading Digital: Turning Technology into Business Transformation* and SVP and Global Practice Lead, Digital Transformation, Capgemini Consulting

So, your digital business transformation got stuck? This excellent book shows you the way forward.

— **Rolf Dobelli,** author of *The Art of Thinking Clearly*

As I read this book, I found myself nodding in agreement and scribbling down ideas at so many moments that were virtual playbacks of my own experiences as a transformation practitioner at Citi. Orchestrating Transformation is a powerful work that should be on the reading list of any executive serious about executing business transformation for results."

— **Amy Radin,** author of *The Change Maker's Playbook: How to Seek, Seed and Scale Innovation In Any Company*

A brilliant book! It demonstrates that digital transformation is not only about the tools, but even more importantly, about the means and the strategy. For all of us tasked with making it happen, it provides an excellent methodology based on practical cases.

— **Fred Herren,** senior vice president of digital and innovation, SGS

In 1951, Lyons started the digital transformation journey with the first business application. New technologies, such as the internet, mobile phones, and AI, each depressed the digital transformation pedal a bit harder so that now the pace of change challenges nearly every organization. Orchestrating Transformation *is a very timely compendium of frameworks for planning digital transformation and the collective wisdom of many senior executives on how to execute required changes. As digital transformation has no brake pedal, you should read this book to stay on the road to the future of business.*

— **Rick Watson,** author of *Electronic Commerce: The Strategic Perspective* and J. Rex Fuqua distinguished chair for internet strategy, University of Georgia

"Digital transformation" is a process and not a goal in itself. Reading the Global Center for Digital Business Transformation's new book **Orchestrating Transformation** *is like a déjà vu of what our clients experience day by day. The book gives very practicable and actionable tips on how to deal with the different aspects of transformation.*

— **Holger Greif,** head of digital at PwC Switzerland

Orchestrating Transformation *is a must-read for executives who are looking for practical tools to succeed in their digital journeys. Based on research and practical experience from IMD's Global Center for Digital Business Transformation, the book provides the frameworks and capabilities required to succeed in a digital transformation. In the jungle of many books and articles about digital, this book stands out with its down-to-earth approach based on a wealth of experience and research about failures and successes.*

— **Carlos Cordon,** author of *Strategy Is Digital: How Companies Can Use Big Data in the Value Chain*

Orchestrating Transformation focuses on the execution challenge of digital transformation, which is at the core of the struggle in many businesses today. While much has been written about the "why" and "what" of digital business transformation, the authors explicitly address the important and pressing "how" question. I consider this book a great source of inspiration, particularly for practitioners whose job it is to successfully drive digital transformation for their companies.

— **Nils Urbach,** author of *IT Management in the Digital Age*

This book addresses one of the biggest business challenges of our time—digital transformation. The team at the Global Center for Digital Business Transformation addresses the several elements of that challenge in the context of today's rapidly changing technology and society. A persuasive case has been made on how business leaders can continually reinvent their companies. I find the case studies compelling and the principles vital for business leaders.

— **Howard Yu,** author of *LEAP: How to Thrive in a World Where Everything Can Be Copied*

Orchestrating Transformation is a must-read for those leading digital transformation as well as those trying to understand the enablers of change for an organization at a time when the speed of change and uncertainty are unprecedented. The value of this book is the practical and illustrative way that the authors address transformation challenges, using examples that are relevant and relatable to the managerial challenges faced, whatever the type of organization. This latest book builds on and takes to the next level the concepts developed in **Digital Vortex,** providing a methodology to help practitioners understand key areas on which to focus, as well as the synergies and connectedness needed to bring effective transformation.

— **Charlotte Lindsey-Curtet,** director of digital transformation, International Committee of the Red Cross (ICRC)

Today, we all face the continuous challenge of digital transformation. *Orchestrating Transformation* provides an actionable and concrete guide to understand how to respond to this challenge through a combination of digital triggers and organizational instruments.

— **Antonio Carriero,** chief digital officer, Breitling

Orchestrating Transformation is an essential read for every leader facing the challenges of developing–and critically executing–a digital strategy. The metaphor of "transformation through orchestration" is a powerful framework for organizing and guiding the process to a successful conclusion. The supporting concepts and tools provide a clear roadmap for implementation.

— **Michael Watkins,** author of *The First 90 Days: Proven Strategies for Getting Up to Speed Faster and Smarter*

The missing link in digital transformation is neither "digital" nor "transformation" but, rather, detailed insights about how to make the two work together. *Orchestrating Transformation* goes right to the heart of the managerial issues that can make or break any transformation effort. It blends data-driven business logic with vivid, live illustrations to provide clarity on which choices must be made, why, and how best to do it. The book restores faith in why business research is essential to make business cases relevant.

— **Bill Fischer,** author of *Reinventing Giants: How Chinese Global Competitor Haier Has Changed the Way Big Companies Transform*

Today's digital economy, driven by Internet of Things technologies, not only reverberates throughout all industries, but throughout the multilayered interactions of each organization. However, many business leaders and their companies are struggling to adjust to these new realities. Traditional, linear change management practices no longer work. In *Orchestrating Transformation,* the authors provide a score sheet for successfully orchestrating transformation in today's digital world–covering everything from implementing new processes, strategies, and technologies to company culture, customer relationships, and job skills. In practical steps, this book shows leaders which "entangled" problems to focus on, and then explains how to untangle them to ensure their companies thrive amid our fast-changing times.

— **Maciej Kranz,** vice president of strategic innovation, Cisco, and author of *Building the Internet of Things*

Orchestrating Transformation rightfully recognizes that a digital transformation is, in fact, not about "digital." Instead, it requires all aspects that make up a business to sing in harmony. The book successfully connects realistic digital transformation challenges to a practical, end-to-end approach to deliver results.

— **Tom Voskes,** CEO of SparkOptimus and author of *Make Disruption Work: a CEO Handbook for Digital Transformation*

This book is about learning from failure—what everyone is consistently getting wrong about digital transformation, and how to fix it. The authors critically rethink traditional approaches to change management and provide a fresh perspective on transformation. Based on rigorous research and full of interesting, real-life examples, *Orchestrating Transformation* is a must-read for every manager involved in transformation. You will find a practical guide for how to orchestrate large-scale organizational changes with clear actions and recommendations. If you read only one book per year, I would recommend you choose this one.

— **Anna Drobakha,** chief marketing officer at Avito

The new book *Orchestrating Transformation* has given me both inspiration and very practical tooling in our own transformation at Rabobank. Transforming an organization is indeed a constant "orchestration" of capabilities, tooling, and, not to forget, culture. **Orchestrating Transformation** is a great read for everyone responsible for, and involved in, digital transformation.

— **Bart Leurs,** chief digital transformation officer, Rabobank

Orchestrating Transformation breaks down the greatest and most hyped transformation challenge faced by the leadership of any modern business today. In doing so, the authors deliver a clear, pragmatic set of guidelines and tools that anyone serious about succeeding in their digital transformation efforts needs to apply.

— **Dominic Weir,** chief digital officer, IWC Schaffhausen

ORCHESTRATING TRANSFORMATION

How to Deliver Winning Performance with a Connected Approach to Change

Michael Wade · James Macaulay
Andy Noronha · Joel Barbier

ORCHESTRATING TRANSFORMATION

How to Deliver Winning Performance with a Connected Approach to Change

Michael Wade, James Macaulay, Andy Noronha, and Joel Barbier

ISBN: 978-1-945010-05-7

To Heidi, the perfect partner through life's transformations.
– M.W.

To Jenn, Ellen, Cameron, and Carol, my most valuable connections.
– J.M.

To my parents, Pascal and Sunita, who have shown me that there can be no adventure without change.
– A.N.

To my wife, Rebecca, and my children, Anna, Hélène, Raphaël, and Claire, you are my inspiration and strength.
– J.B.

TABLE OF CONTENTS

INTRODUCTION
The Context for Transformation

A NEW ASSIGNMENT

On November 15, 2017, Ann-Christin Andersen received an unexpected job offer: she was asked to become her company's first chief digital officer (CDO). TechnipFMC was a $15 billion oil and gas field services organization, with 37,000 employees in 48 countries, whose lines of business included building refineries and installing pumps and pipes on the sea floor.

The link to digital was not obvious to her. Further, she wasn't even sure what the role entailed or why she had been tapped to take it on. Andersen had never worked in IT or the high-tech sector. Though she was an engineer by training, most of her experience had been on the commercial side of the organization, most recently as managing director of TechnipFMC's Norwegian business, one of the company's largest.

While she was familiar with the CDO title—it was hard to miss the hype surrounding digital technologies and their disruptive effects—she had little idea what a CDO actually did. And she wasn't sure if TechnipFMC's top management team, who had made her the offer, knew either.

After a bit of digging, Andersen learned that the company had recently lost a few large bids, due in part to its lack of digital capabilities and a clear digital strategy. This customer feedback had come as a surprise to senior management. TechnipFMC was a recognized leader in the market and a trusted partner for many of the world's largest oil and gas players. Digital tools, analytics, and applications had never figured prominently in an industry dominated by mechanical technologies and systems. So for TechnipFMC to be losing deals on the basis of inadequate *digital* capabilities sent shockwaves through the company's leadership.

Intrigued, Andersen accepted the position. Then came the hard part—what to do next. Her responsibilities weren't clear, and she had no team, budget, or defined set of objectives.

Andersen's situation is not uncommon. Today, senior executives see digital opportunities and threats, and feel the need to act. Even if they are in a strong market position, they worry that a new competitor, technology, or business model could instantly upend the dynamics of their industry.

They're right to feel anxious.

During the first wave of digital disruption, the hardest-hit industries were those where the core product or service could be readily digitized, namely media and entertainment, financial services, telecommunications, and high tech. Companies in these industries have had to build new capabilities, shift resources and structures, and reconstruct legacy businesses.

Some have been successful. Others have fallen by the wayside.

Now, a second wave of disruption is upon us. This wave is focused not only on digitizing products and services, but also on business models, processes, and value chains. As a result, it's not just crashing onto industries prone to the digitization of offerings. It's also affecting sectors that offer physical products, as well as companies operating in the business-to-business (B2B) realm—companies like TechnipFMC.

TechnipFMC is a fairly representative B2B player. It offers services to large companies in the oil and gas industry. It doesn't find the gas but helps to move it from where it is to where it needs to go next. It doesn't refine the oil, but helps to build, commission, and maintain the refineries that do. The company concentrates on specialized work, often complicated and dirty, with long timelines and thin margins.

It's a tough business, but a relatively stable one. In a world where many organizations are concerned about being "Uberized" or "Amazoned," the space in which TechnipFMC operates is unlikely to disappear. The business environment has seen few new entrants and no "digital giants" (there is no Netflix—yet—in the oil and gas field services sector). Traditionally, the biggest worry for TechnipFMC has been the price of oil, which influences its customers' investments and, therefore, its own revenues and profits.

Despite this, the company was being told in no uncertain terms by its customers that it must think more deeply about digitization. Otherwise, it would lose business to competitors. So, the need to change was clear. *How* to change was not.

Like many business leaders facing the task of company transformation, Andersen was feeling lost. As a successful executive, this was not a familiar emotion. In her previous roles, she had dealt with a lot of complexity, but it was manageable complexity.

In her new position, she wasn't comfortable at all. For starters, she didn't understand much about digital technologies. As an oil and gas engineer, she was more versed in compact manifolds and flexible jumpers than in cloud computing or augmented reality.

Worse, she was unsure of her remit or how her performance would be assessed. And she wasn't clear on the extent of senior management's engagement and support for this initiative. They were interested enough in digital to create her position, but were they really committed to a wholesale transformation? And would they give her the means to transform the organization?

Andersen's biggest fear was that she would become what she herself called the "Queen of PowerPoint." In other words, she would do a lot of talking, and create a lot of slides featuring words like "strategy" and "enablement," but people in the business would largely ignore her. Coming from the business herself, she fully recognized the danger of becoming a corporate irrelevance.

THE BIG QUESTION: HOW?

We wrote this book for all the Ann-Christin Andersens out there.

These are the people who've been tapped on the shoulder and told something like, "We want you to drive our digital transformation," or

"We would like you to build up our digital capability," or "Could you help us to find new ways to make money through digital?"

The DBT Center's latest research (see the sidebar, "About Us") with 1,030 executives from around the world found that 65 percent of large and midsized organizations have hired a chief digital officer. (Of course, not all digital executives wear this title. They may be called "head of digital" or "VP of transformation," or they may not have a new title at all.)

About Us

The Global Center for Digital Business Transformation (DBT Center), an IMD and Cisco Initiative, was officially opened on June 23, 2015. Based in Lausanne, Switzerland, on the campus of IMD, one of the world's top-ranked business schools, the DBT Center comprises researchers from both of its founding entities: IMD and Cisco, the Silicon Valley-based high-tech leader. Our research focuses on digital disruption, business model innovation, and transformation-oriented themes involving people, process, and technology change. Executives come to the DBT Center to grapple with and innovate around their most pressing business challenges.

Transformation, we've discovered, is a job that influences virtually all leadership roles in large organizations. In most cases, however, those who are tasked with executing a digital business transformation are set up to fail. And this failure is rooted in how the assignment is framed at the outset. Most digital business transformations focus on the "digital," when what they really need to focus on is the "business transformation."

Our last book, *Digital Vortex: How Today's Market Leaders Can Beat Disruptive Competitors at Their Own Game,* delved deeply into the "why" and the "what" of digital business transformation. In its introduction, though, we made clear that *Digital Vortex* was "not a book that is, strictly speaking, about 'transformation'—at least not in the classic sense of the word." We intended it not as a blueprint for transformation per se, but as we wrote then, as a "manual for how to compete."

Today, executing a digital business transformation is the pressing business challenge that preoccupies leaders, which is why we tackle it here in *Orchestrating Transformation: How to Deliver Winning Performance with a Connected Approach to Change.*

"How do we begin?" "How do we define success?" "How do we construct our roadmap?" These are the questions this book will address. It's designed for "practitioners" whose job is to drive digital business transformation—significant, strategic, at scale—for their companies. It is *not* a general book about digitization, technology, or garden-variety organizational change.

UPDATE FROM THE DIGITAL VORTEX

When we formed the DBT Center in 2015 and began our deep-dive research and client engagement on digital disruption, we quickly recognized its potential to reshape competitive landscapes and deeply affect the future of all industries. As we reviewed the data we had gathered, the metaphor of a vortex emerged for us to help describe the market change we were observing.

A vortex, like a tornado or whirlpool, exerts a rotational force on objects around it, drawing them toward its center. The Digital Vortex is the market context of disruption, characterized by an irresistible force that pulls all organizations toward a point where "everything that can be digitized is digitized." Offerings, business models, and value chains become digitized, and physical components that inhibit competitive advantage (e.g., legacy investments, physical infrastructures, and manual processes) are cast off. In a vortex, objects often break apart from the force of the rotation. That is precisely what is happening to incumbents' value chains—disruptors are unbundling links in the chain with digital technologies and business models that allow them to create new value for customers and market change in the process.

> The Digital Vortex is the market context of disruption, characterized by an irresistible force that pulls all organizations toward a point where "everything that can be digitized is digitized."

As companies are pulled toward the middle of the vortex, where digitization and disruption are most intense, they collide and create new competitive forms; industry convergence, whether between banking and retail or healthcare and telecommunications, becomes the norm. Disruptive companies like Tencent and Amazon are using digital capabilities to quickly cross industry boundaries, blurring the lines between traditional notions of "sectors" and company types.

Executives and transformation practitioners are beginning to recognize the impact of the Digital Vortex phenomenon and what it means for their companies' competitive position. In DBT Center research from 2017, roughly half of executives reported that digital disruption was already happening in meaningful terms in their industries, compared with only 15 percent in 2015 (see Figure 1). Digitally driven market change is also increasingly capturing the attention of C-level executives. In 2015, digital disruption was not deemed worthy of board-level attention in about 45 percent of companies. Just two short years later, only 17 percent felt this way.

Fig. 1: Timeline for Significant Market Change Due to Digital Disruption

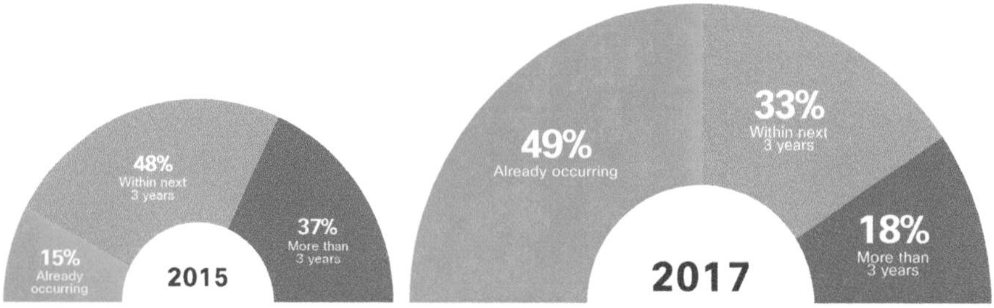

48% Within next 3 years

37% More than 3 years

15% Already occurring

2015

49% Already occurring

33% Within next 3 years

18% More than 3 years

2017

2015 N=941
2017 N=636

Source: Global Center for Digital Business Transformation, 2015-17

More than 30 percent of respondents in 2017 believed that digital disruption would have a transformative impact on their industries. By contrast, less than *1 percent* felt this way back in 2015. Clearly, the avalanche of news stories—e.g., Amazon acquiring its way into the pharmacy industry with the US $1 billion purchase of startup PillPack in June 2018, and the immediate US $12 billion drop in the market capitalization of pharmacy retailers—has served as a wake-up call.[1]

Seventy-five percent of executives now believe that the impact of disruption on their industries is "major" or "transformative," a stark increase in just two years (see Figure 2).

Fig. 2: Perceived Impacts of Digital Disruption on Company's Industry

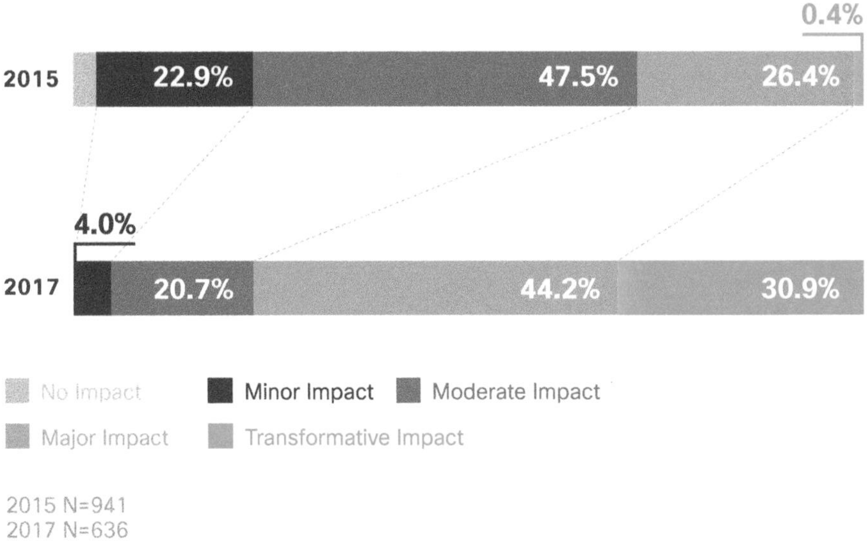

				0.4%
2015	22.9%	47.5%	26.4%	

	4.0%			
2017	20.7%	44.2%	30.9%	

No Impact   **Minor Impact**   Moderate Impact
Major Impact   Transformative Impact

2015 N=941
2017 N=636

Source: Global Center for Digital Business Transformation, 2015-17

Venture capital and private equity placements, moreover, continue to pour into disruptive players at unprecedented rates,[2] and the perceived urgency to transform has never been greater among business leaders.

Organizations' willingness to respond to digital disruption is also improving—if only marginally. In 2015, 25 percent of executives claimed their organizations were actively responding to digital disruption. This number increased to 31 percent in 2017. Nevertheless, 40 percent still felt their companies did not understand digital disruption or were responding inappropriately—only a slight improvement from 2015 (see Figure 3).

Fig. 3: **Level of Company Response to Digital Disruption**

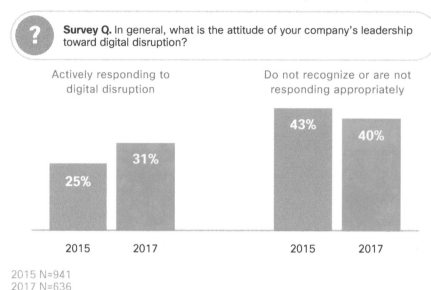

Survey Q. In general, what is the attitude of your company's leadership toward digital disruption?

Actively responding to digital disruption

Do not recognize or are not responding appropriately

| 25% | 31% | 43% | 40% |
| 2015 | 2017 | 2015 | 2017 |

2015 N=941
2017 N=636

Source: Global Center for Digital Business Transformation, 2015-17

The data shows that the pace of digital disruption has accelerated over the past two years. Across industries, executives are feeling its impact more acutely. While their ability to respond has improved with some maturation of digital capabilities, our analysis shows that there's still a large gap between acknowledging the need to transform and actually achieving digital business transformation.

THE DELUSION OF MARKET LEADERS

In *Digital Vortex,* we recommended that incumbents emulate certain things about disruptive competitors (e.g., their ability to create customer value, their level of operational agility). We added, however, that we were not "exalting" disruptors, whether scrappy startups or digital giants like Alibaba and Amazon. In fact, we correctly predicted in 2016 that many of the high-profile startups we profiled would "flame out," either by being acquired or otherwise folding up their tents.

When it comes to digital business transformation, rather than creating competitive change through disruption, startups and digital giants can actually tell us very little. As Joe Miranda, CDO of $11 billion mass media and information services leader Thomson Reuters, noted in our conversation, "Digital natives and cloud-first companies—your Amazon, Airbnb—were born digital. Most of them were born out of a 'garage' with a single code base in a single culture. They weren't born through acquisition. They haven't been in the market for 50 to 100 years, and didn't have to address the burden of significant accumulated technical debt." In other words, when it comes to transformation, disruptive players and incumbents are apples and oranges.

It's therefore risky for incumbents to try to imitate digital giants like Facebook, Amazon, Apple, Netflix, Alibaba, Google, or Tesla. These companies have heaps of management articles and books written about them.[3] However, like Ozymandias, the "king of kings," whose statue lies crumbling in the desert of Shelley's poem, digital giants appear somewhat less formidable than they did two years ago.

Since 2016, for example, Uber has found its path strewn with potholes. Reports about a toxic and discriminatory culture led to the ousting of the CEO in July 2017. Charges of labor abuse toward drivers and battles with regulators dominated the headlines during this period. Between 2016 and 2018, Uber retreated from Russia, China, and Southeast Asia.

Uber is not alone. Facebook has endured what *Wired* called "a hellish two years," drawing the ire of both consumers and government watchdogs. The company's leadership has been consistently on the defensive, combating stories that paint Facebook as a purveyor of "fake news" and prone to privacy breaches. These stories, and others, helped spawn a global mass movement with the name "Delete Facebook."[4]

It's also dangerous to focus too much on successes. Unfortunately, this is what most business books do. They look at successful companies or individuals, describe what they do, extrapolate some "keys" to their success, and then suggest how you can put these "lessons" to work for you.

There are many reasons that companies and people succeed. Often, macro-economic or sectoral forces should get as much credit as anything the company or the individual did. Sometimes, share price is a function of irrational exuberance, as Alan Greenspan called it, or some other factor. For many high-performing market leaders, any business transformation may have been coincidental to success, not the cause of it. Hence, the companies that perform best are not necessarily the most useful examples of how transformation programs should be executed.

As our IMD colleague Phil Rosenzweig noted in his discussion of the Halo Effect:

> The fact is that many everyday concepts in business—including leadership, corporate culture, core competencies, and customer orientation—are ambiguous and difficult to define. We often infer perceptions of them from something else, which appears to be more concrete and tangible: namely, financial performance. As a result, many of the things that we commonly believe are *contributions* to company performance are in fact *attributions.* In other words, outcomes can be mistaken for inputs.[5]

This calls into question the lessons learned from the "best" companies—think *In Search of Excellence or Good to Great*—and how they can be applied to your company. The Halo Effect, the tendency to infer the presence of a successful strategy (or program of digital business transformation) by dint of good financial performance, leads many authors to focus on uncovering the "hidden DNA" of the most innovative or high-performing companies.[6]

This book doesn't do that.

Transformation is not an event; it's an essential and perpetual task of leadership.

Orchestrating Transformation is less about what the best companies do better than anyone else. Instead, it's largely about what everyone gets consistently wrong—and how to fix it. This book proceeds from a simple premise: most companies are not successful in digital business transformation. Our research and experience show that there are no magical structures, no transformation geniuses, no hidden DNA. But there *are* consistencies in what companies do poorly. There *are* lessons we can glean from the common failures to design a successful and executable approach to digital business transformation.

While precise levels of failure in transformation programs remain a source of debate,[7] new studies reveal distressingly low returns on transformation investments.[8] And anecdotal evidence is everywhere about how change is stymied in large organizations.

If your company falls into the small subset of organizations that are great at driving change at scale, this is probably not the book for you. But if your organization is more like those we meet every day—large, mature, prosperous companies that don't know how to successfully drive a digital business transformation, and have tried repeatedly with mixed or no results—then the frameworks and tools in *Orchestrating Transformation* may help.

COMPANIES ARE NOT CATERPILLARS

When we embarked on the research that gave rise to *Digital Vortex,* it quickly became apparent that while digital disruption was a buzzword, there had been no in-depth investigation of how the disruption actually happened. Our second major research project taught us that, in the same vein, when it comes to digital business transformation, platitudes abound. Did you know, for example, that "data is the new oil"? Or that "software is eating the world"? Empty wisdoms like these don't shed much light on the mechanisms of digital business transformation.

In the two years between the publication of *Digital Vortex* and this book, a startling finding surfaced: executives fundamentally misunderstand transformation in the context of today's large organizations.

First, too many companies see transformation as a kind of momentary revolution, or more commonly, as an episode they must endure, emerging on the other side of the process in an altered state. Like a caterpillar, the organization undergoes a one-time metamorphosis and, if the change works, it emerges from the chrysalis as a beautiful butterfly. Now, the organism can do things that no mere caterpillar ever could.

This analogy is misguided and hinders incumbents from successfully executing transformation programs. Transformation is not an event; it's an essential and *perpetual* task of leadership. To quote Ben Franklin, "When you're finished changing, you're finished."

As Figure 4 shows, executives surveyed by the DBT Center recognize that business model reinvention will not happen over generations, or every few decades, but rather every few years. And for roughly a quarter of companies, those that find themselves on a high-speed trajectory toward the center of the Digital Vortex, it's an annual requirement. Yet their thinking on transformation remains more monolithic—*we have to buckle down and get through this period of transition.*

Second, we've found that few leaders grasp the *connected nature of change.* Executives need to think about organizational change in a radically different light. Much like digital disruption, companies across the board feel the challenge of connectedness, but don't know how to cope with it, harness it, or turn it to their advantage.

When addressing the question of "how?", one quickly encounters an inherent level-of-analysis problem: on one end, being so high level that prescriptions are meaningless; on the other, too complex and granular to be of general utility in a range of settings. In the former, we've come to believe firmly there is no cookie-cutter approach that spells out "how you do digital transformation." In the latter, too much granularity—or said another way, the lack of a holistic

Definition of Digital Business Transformation

We define digital business transformation as "organizational change through the use of digital technologies and business models to improve performance." First, the objective of digital business transformation is to improve business performance. Second, digital business transformation is based on a digital foundation. Organizations are continually transforming, but to qualify as a digital business transformation, one or more digital technologies must exert a significant influence. Third, digital business transformation requires organizational change—change that includes processes, people, and strategy. In sum, digital business transformation involves much more than technology.

approach—is the root cause that gives rise to such high rates of failure. This holistic approach must recognize that digital is a means to help transform a business, rather than an end in itself (see sidebar, "Definition of Digital Business Transformation").

Fig. 4: **Frequency of Business Model Reinvention**

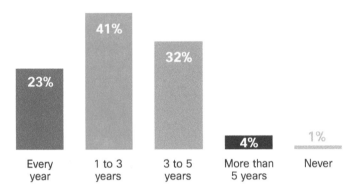

 Survey Q. In the future, how often do you think your organization will be forced by competitive pressures to reinvent its business model (e.g., how it makes money, how it offers value to customers)?

N=1,030

Source: Global Center for Digital Business Transformation, 2019

In this book, we use the concept of *orchestration* to contend with the connected nature of change. We find inspiration and practical applications of how to orchestrate in a range of fields. By embracing the *networked* nature of organizations, and the challenge of changing what is

Note: Appendix 4 provides an actionable summary of 21 of our most critical recommendations for transformation practitioners.

highly connected, we reframe what the execution of a digital business transformation program means (continuous and holistic) and increase the chances that it will ultimately succeed.

THE STRUCTURE OF THIS BOOK

Throughout *Orchestrating Transformation,* we provide real-world stories of how organizations have taken a connected approach to their transformation programs (or, in some cases, failed to do so). Along the way, we lay out specific direction and executable tools that, when assembled, constitute a methodology for how to orchestrate large-scale organizational change, including four appendices at the back of the book with tools for practitioners.

In the first chapter, we detail three organizational characteristics of today's market incumbents—scale, interdependence, and dynamism—and show why the "entanglement" of these characteristics makes it nearly impossible to achieve success in digital business transformation using traditional change methods. We call this the "transformation dilemma" of today's incumbents.

Borrowing from other disciplines like ecology, climatology, and urban planning, we show how orchestration has addressed similar challenges in other settings. For years, a lot of smart people have been thinking about how to orchestrate in domains outside of management and digital business transformation. What can they tell us?

We explain what it means to orchestrate—"to mobilize and enable so as to achieve a desired effect"—and how a mindset focused on connectedness enables firms to address transformation challenges in a profoundly new way, operating in what we term the "Orchestration Zone."

Chapter 2 provides a recap of some key concepts from *Digital Vortex,* including customer value creation, business models, and our Strategic Response Playbook. Note that several important ideas and frameworks from our earlier book are discussed in this one as well. We view these two bodies of work as a tandem that provides prescriptive insights for practitioners—first on how to create the organizational *capacity for change,* and now on the *mechanics of executing change.*

Chapter 3 addresses the crucial issue of setting the company's strategic direction and the context for its transformation. Getting this right is necessary for successful transformation. No matter how perfectly a program may be executed, if the business model and strategy are wrong, the transformation will be a dud. We chart how organizations must conceive and enact clear "guiding objectives" that prioritize customer value creation, and a "transformation ambition" that can galvanize efforts across the business.

In Chapter 4, we present the conceptual anchoring of the book, the *Transformation Orchestra*. Conceiving of the organization as a symphony orchestra made up of "instruments"–the organizational resources it needs to bring to bear to drive change–allows us to frame the execution of organizational change in an entirely new light.

We maintain that every major transformation challenge practitioners face– whether that be creating a new customer experience or changing company culture–is an intrinsically networked activity that involves many different organizational resources working together. These resources include the people, data, and infrastructure of the company. Organizational resources aligned to address a particular challenge are what we refer to as a *transformation network,* a key construct that allows the organization to move quickly, and in lockstep, marshaling resources from wherever they might reside in the organization.

In Chapter 5, we explore what it means for the agents of change to orchestrate in this context–mobilizing resources and enabling their connections–through a series of concrete activities, driven by

The Research

Research was foundational to the insights in *Orchestrating Transformation*. It included secondary and primary research, and was supported by research partners Cicero Group, Evalueserve, the Gerson Lehrman Group, and Lightspeed Research.

First, extensive secondary research went into formulating the broad theme of the book: orchestration. Beginning in May 2017, the DBT Center studied the literature on change management and organizational behavior. We combed management journals, business press, and IT-focused sources for examples of companies undergoing transformations, both successes and failures. Further reading on each of those organizations, in some cases supplemented by executive interviews, allowed the authors to compare them based on the challenges they were facing and how they were organizing for change.

The DBT Center also conducted an online survey to uncover more widely: 1) the

(Continued on next page)

The Research

(Continued from previous page)

challenges organizations are facing as they transform their business models and organizations; 2) their capacity to manage change; and 3) how they are organized to execute a transformation.

In total, we surveyed 1,030 director-level-and-above executives worldwide, in both private and public organizations with a minimum of 500 employees. The survey was conducted across 14 countries and in 11 languages in mid-2018.

Finally, dozens of in-depth interviews with transformation practitioners were the most important source of enlightenment, as well as the stories featured in the book.

the orchestrator. Here, we describe eight "orchestration competencies" needed to mobilize resources and enable the connections between them. Building these competencies is a clear call-to-action for transformation practitioners.

In Chapter 6, we examine how companies should organize themselves to drive strong orchestration. We explore how transformation programs are governed in large and midsized organizations, including who acts as the "orchestrator," the person who "conducts" the Transformation Orchestra and is responsible for how the transformation program is executed. We describe the orchestrator's charter and the responsibilities of the transformation office he or she leads.

We recommend moving past a conventional functional orientation to a connected "organizational fabric" overlaid on the existing company hierarchy. This more agile organizational construct helps mobilize resources and enable connections dynamically, fostering good execution in the company's transformation efforts. Finally, we delve further into transformation networks and what they mean for executing organizational change, and explain how they work in a networked and agile way, drawing resources from across the business to create new processes and better capabilities.

In the book's conclusion, we revisit many of our core ideas and offer our final thoughts on taking a connected approach to organizational change. We provide an executable orchestration-centric approach to transformation that practitioners can use, relying on the example of a fictitious company and how they put the tenets and frameworks of *Or-*

chestrating Transformation into action. Throughout, we highlight steps companies should take that reflect the best practices uncovered in our research for taking a connected approach to change.

Finally, we look to what innovations like artificial intelligence (AI) and blockchain portend for digital business transformations and how they will be undertaken in the future. In the book's epilogue, we check back with Ann-Christin Andersen to see how things are progressing on TechnipFMC's transformation journey.

A DISPATCH FROM THE FRONT LINES

Orchestrating Transformation is the product of more than two years of research on how to execute a digital business transformation (see sidebar, "The Research"). Although we devoted plenty of energy to running surveys, tabulating statistics, and immersing ourselves in the literature on organizational change, much of the learning that went into this book came from workshops and teaching programs with executives who were wrestling with digital transformations themselves.

In the intervening three years between the publication of *Digital Vortex* and *Orchestrating Transformation,* the people who make up the DBT Center (from both IMD and Cisco) have met with or held briefings or executive education sessions with leaders from more than 1,000 organizations to discuss digital disruption and the challenges they're facing. We ran more than 20 cohorts of IMD's Leading Digital Business Transformation and other digitally focused open-enrollment programs, and delivered multi-customer workshops on six continents. All told, in keeping with the DBT Center's charter of applied research, we estimate that we've presented our frameworks and discussed their application with more than 10,000 executives around the globe.

Throughout it all, we've engaged with a multitude of companies undergoing transformations, with wide-ranging discrepancies in terms of experience and outcomes. In many cases, these seminars and executive workshops were the incubator for our concepts, spurring us to address the question of "how?" They also allowed us to road-test our frameworks and adjust them as we collected more data and feedback: Do they make sense? Do they have explanatory power? Can a company implement them?

This book is therefore a kind of dispatch from the front lines. Indeed, many of the companies we interviewed for *Orchestrating Transformation* were identified after discussions with their executives revealed they had learned some hard-won lessons on how to transform. We believe other companies can also benefit from these lessons.

CHAPTER 1
The Transformation Dilemma

ENTANGLED INCUMBENTS

The vast majority of organizational change efforts fail. Estimates vary, but failure rates range from 60 to 80 percent and don't seem to improve over time.[1]

And when it comes to *digital* transformations, recent research suggests that a paltry 5 percent meet or exceed expectations.[2] In fact, digital transformations fail so frequently that we've met many executives who are hostile to the very term "digital," or who have made any phrases containing "transformation" *verboten* because of the word's perceived connotations of hype, frustration, and fiasco.

On some level, reservations about the word "transformation" stem from a discomfort with change and the turbulence it causes. There's good reason. The truth is that, despite our labors as managers, as with the universe itself, the level of disorder within organizations never decreases (in physics, this is known as the second law of thermodynamics).

The natural state of companies as they grow and mature is always towards more disorder. The word people use to take the measure of disorder in any system is "entropy." This word derives from the English prefix *en-*, meaning "internal," and the Greek word τροπή, pronounced *"tropē,"* which has an interesting etymology. It means "transformation."

As noted, one of the main reasons for this transformation failure rate is that many company leaders don't understand the problem they face. This misunderstanding flows from three organizational characteristics that, together, stack the odds against digital transformation success when traditional change methods are used:

1. **Scale.** Companies are awash in huge volumes of "things that need to be managed": tasks, budgets, planning cycles, organizational changes. In addition to the *number* of things to be managed, there are also many *different* things that must be managed: processes, data, systems, assets, structures, and people. Companies face an acute case of information overload as well. The data is not merely "big" in volume, but also high in variety.

2. **Interdependence.** The things that need to be managed are interrelated, and the effects from any one action are felt *throughout* the organization in ways that aren't easy to predict.

3. **Dynamism.** The things that need to be managed, and the environments (market, regulatory, etc.) in which they operate, are constantly evolving. The need to do things differently is a constant competitive reality. Simply put: things change a lot.

Because these characteristics go hand in hand and reinforce each other, we refer to them as the organization's level of ***entanglement*** (see Figure 5).

Fig. 5: **Organizational Entanglement**

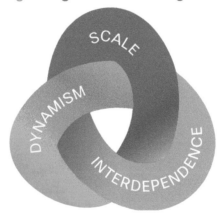

Source: Global Center for Digital Business Transformation, 2019

In *Digital Vortex,* we coined the phrase "encumbered incumbents" to describe the challenge large and midsized companies face in adapting to disruptive competition. We noted that they are "saddled with cost structures and value chains tuned to the competitive dynamics of an earlier era." These structures and value chains encumber companies' efforts to compete. *Entangled* incumbents are hobbled in their efforts to *transform*.

Our interactions with companies worldwide tell us that a new approach to digital business transformation is needed—one that acknowledges this entanglement.

SCALE: MORE, MORE, MORE

Imagine that two computers each store information. The first contains information in amount X; the second has information in amount Y. Now let's suppose that the information on these two devices is needed by different parts of the organization at different times and for different reasons. (It would be easy to imagine the computers as servers containing employee data, for example.)

From the organization's standpoint, the total volume of information is not merely the sum of the information on the two machines (X + Y). Additional information is required to understand how the information on one machine *relates* to that on the other. Is the information duplicative? Is it contradictory?

The organization may also need to know: its location; whether it's properly secured; whether it's accurate; when it was produced; who has access to it; how other parts of the business use it; what the data can tell us about other information we possess, and so on.

Now imagine this situation playing out across an entire organization with thousands of information stores, users, and scenarios in which the information is needed. We all know information in companies is growing rapidly (as in "Big Data"), but less attention has been paid to this organizational metadata, which is a mainspring of execution complexity. In short, information *about* information is a natural byproduct of organizational scale.

When Ann-Christin Andersen first started asking her colleagues about the digital maturity of TechnipFMC, she was told variations of a similar story: the company had a few ongoing efforts, but mostly there wasn't much happening on digital. She decided to put this to the test by taking a quick inventory of the company's digital initiatives.

The results shocked her. While the company's customers had called out a lack of digital capability, she nonetheless quickly uncovered more than 180 digital initiatives in various stages of completion. They were scattered across the company's three major business units and in shared service organizations such as IT, HR, and finance. Very few of the people in charge of the initiatives were aware of the others, even in cases where the work significantly overlapped in scope.

Andersen quickly realized that she'd need to get a handle on the abundance and diversity of these initiatives. Volume is one thing, but diversity can heighten problems of organizational entanglement.

Eventually, she discovered that the different digital projects, even those tackling the same challenges, were using different underlying standards, protocols, and technologies. Sometimes, identical problems were being addressed in different parts of the company in totally different ways. A lot of projects couldn't leave the pilot stage.

Does this sound familiar?

INTERDEPENDENCE: HITCHED TO EVERYTHING ELSE

The complexity that comes from managing "many things" and "different things" can be made worse when those things are connected to—and affect—one another.

"There's a lot of interdependence amongst capabilities within our organization, and that interdependence has such a huge effect," said Michael Loughlean, director of enterprise architecture at Suncor, a $28 billion Canadian integrated energy giant. "In fact, we can understand more from the dependencies than we can from the work that we're actually trying to get done.

"For example, we looked at the dependencies just within what we call 'reliability enablement,'" Loughlean explained. "We came up with 40 business capabilities that you need to be good at in order to do reliability well. But we also came up with 28 *other* capabilities that reliability was actually dependent upon—capabilities that came from other areas. So you've got to be able to say, 'This is a great initiative, but because of those dependencies, let's not forget these other three, four groups that need to be a part of things.'"

In his seminal 1967 book *Organizations in Action,* American sociologist James D. Thompson described three types of interdependence, which are illustrated in Figure 6. Each demands a different approach to management and "coordinating" activities.

Fig. 6: Three Types of Interdependence

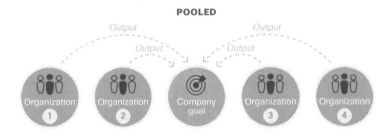

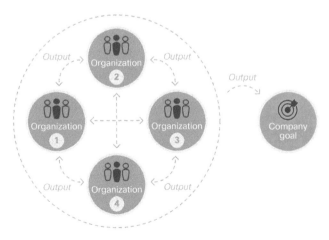

Source: Global Center for Digital Business Transformation, 2019

The first is *sequential interdependence.* Here, Thompson described a situation akin to an assembly line, where the outputs of a given group serve as the inputs of another. Groups are interdependent because each depends on other groups farther up the chain. The coordination that this style of interdependence requires is what we consider "planning" (e.g., scheduling the timing of tasks, arranging the position of resources to accomplish a task).

The second form is *pooled interdependence.* Pooled interdependence occurs when everyone is doing discrete, but often similar, tasks in parallel that somehow "roll up" to a larger goal. A sales team can be thought of as exhibiting pooled interdependence. The form of coordination that matches pooled interdependence is "standardization." For example, by standardizing how salespeople submit orders or report their pipeline, their outputs can be combined to achieve the collective task of revenue growth.

Finally, Thompson's third form of interdependence is what he called *reciprocal interdependence.* Here, teams may be sequentially interdependent, but a change made by one team impacts the work of all other teams. There is a high level of interaction across groups. Inputs and outputs can be cyclical and even flow in different directions (meaning I use your output and you use mine). We can say a company's finance and IT departments are reciprocally interdependent: the former supports the latter, and the latter supports the former. This type of interdependence best reflects the reality within most large organizations today.

The type of coordination called for in instances of reciprocal interdependence is "mutual adjustment"[3]: whenever you make a change, I need to know about it, and vice versa. However, maintaining this awareness, and then adapting based on that information, takes an inordinate toll on an organization.

In his 1996 bestseller *Leading Change,* John Kotter helped us visualize what transformation entails when reciprocal interdependence is the norm. Kotter asked us to imagine walking into an office. Once inside, we decide we don't like the way the room is arranged. With a few easy steps—shifting the location of chairs, bringing in a different desk, rehanging some artwork—the appearance of the office changes quickly. This type of change is straightforward.

He then posited a very different type of office:

> Now imagine going into another office where a series of ropes, big rubber bands, and steel cables connect the objects to one another. First, you'd have trouble even walking into the room without getting tangled up. After making your way slowly over to the chair, you try to move it, but find that this lightweight piece of furniture won't budge. Straining harder, you do move the chair a few inches, but then you notice that a dozen books have been pulled off the bookshelf and that the sofa has also moved slightly in a direction you don't like. You slowly work your way over to the sofa and try to push it back into the right spot, which turns out to be incredibly difficult. After thirty minutes, you succeed, but now a lamp has been pulled off the edge of the desk and is precariously hanging in mid-air, supported by a cable going in one direction and a rope going in another.[4]

This characterization of interdependence is not far from the reality faced by most large companies. You can see how difficult change is in a context like this, and how vexing it is to know where and how hard to push (or pull). As naturalist John Muir wrote in his memoir *My First Summer in the Sierra,* "When we try to pick out anything by itself, we find it hitched to everything else in the Universe."[5]

Often, companies respond to interdependence by separating things into different units. This approach, known as "departmentalization," gives a certain team the authority to establish ("own") a standard for how something is done. At first glance, the approach makes sense as an antidote for complexity. However, it also contributes to the balkanization of companies (i.e., silos), undermining the biggest *value* of interdependence: *synergy.* It's funny that we don't like interdependence in companies when it creates complexity, yet we can't live without the synergy that comes with more integration and interdependence. A lack of synergy is a

A lack of synergy is a major contributing factor in why most transformation programs fail to deliver their expected returns.

major contributing factor in why most transformation programs fail to deliver their expected returns.

Figure 7 shows that complexity and synergy can be thought of as the yin and yang of organizational change: two interrelated elements, representing both a duality (two different things) and a unity (a single joint phenomenon).

Fig. 7: The Yin and Yang of Organizational Change

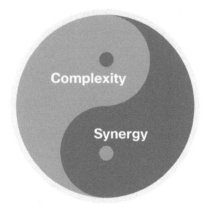

Source: Global Center for Digital Business Transformation, 2019

We've observed that transformation programs usually focus on coordination mechanisms for the two simpler forms of interdependence (sequential and pooled) by stressing planning and standardization. Less frequently do companies recognize the need for mutual adjustment or have any notion of how to do it.

DYNAMISM: THE ONLY CONSTANT IS CHANGE

Scale and interdependence would be hard enough to manage in a static world. But today's environment is anything but static. The speed of change has never been greater, and it's likely to accelerate as the Digital Vortex gains momentum.

The $5 billion Liechtenstein-based power tool manufacturer Hilti has a reputation as an innovator. For example, it was the first in the industry to offer tools-as-a-service to professional tradespeople. However, even innovators have trouble keeping up with the pace of change.

Jean-Louis Keraudren, head of digital integration & e-commerce, described the situation as follows:

> There is still the feeling in our senior management that we are not fast enough. We spend a lot and still we are not fast enough. You can criticize why Hilti is not always number one on the Google ranking. You can criticize why we don't offer Apple Pay for invoices to customers, et cetera. That's why this year we made a big effort to review where we are, what we want to achieve, and distinguish between quick fixes and more fundamental topics like governance and reorganization.

In static systems, component parts are constructed from an initial design. Once the system is in place, it usually doesn't change. Architecture is a static system. The components of buildings change very little over time—or at least very slowly. The roof may need to be repaired or replaced, but the level of dynamism is limited. Interdependencies are well defined, and the pace of evolution is slow. Therefore, these static systems, and the interdependencies they encompass, do a poor job of describing how most organizations operate today.

The Digital Vortex is an external competitive force that is a major engine of dynamism in organizations. But there is another driver of dynamism that is distinctly internal to organizations: adaptation. Dynamic systems (motor vehicle traffic flows, financial markets, insect colonies, companies) are made up of individual units (drivers, investors, ants, employees) that interact with one another and adapt their behaviors based on the actions of other individuals and the state of the system overall.

Even small stimuli can create very large change in the wider system.[6] Think of one car among a hundred thousand breaking down and blocking a lane of traffic. This small-scale disturbance could affect the commutes of everyone in an entire metropolitan region—travel patterns could change extensively and quickly. Constant adaptation by individuals and groups in organizations, a manifestation of interdependence, contributes to dynamism.

By the same token, a large stimulus may have a surprisingly small effect on a dynamic system. For example, a central banker might enact a monetary policy to stem a currency crisis in an economy, but find it has little effect as investors adapt their behaviors based on their own self-interests and expectations about how other factors will impact the currency's value. Similarly, an executive might undertake an ambitious program of digital transformation in his or her company, only to see it come to nothing as the workforce adapts in ways that thwart its aims.

Where can we look to understand dynamic systems? Examples are found in fields such as ecology, biology, climatology, and other natural sciences. These systems are often marked by millions or billions of individual parts, organized into subsystems. The interdependence within these vast, dynamic systems is highly complex, and it morphs rapidly. These systems far better describe today's companies: they are much like living organisms—always changing, and always highly variable and complex.

TALES OF THE UNEXPECTED

In fact, nature contains many systems that possess all three aspects of entanglement. Natural ecosystems, huge in scale (in terms of both the amount and variety of plant and animal life), contain numerous, diverse, and interdependent elements. They are also constantly changing.

One example involves the return of the gray wolf to Yellowstone National Park.[7] By 1926, all gray wolves, the natural "apex predator" in Yellowstone, had been exterminated. In the mid-1990s, gray wolves were reintroduced into the park, and scientists soon observed how their predatory habits affected the entire food chain and overall biodiversity of the region.

The reintroduced gray wolves killed and ate the park's elk population. In turn, the reduced number of grazing elk allowed for the growth of more vegetation. This increase in plant life and its root systems then increased the stability of riverbanks and, ultimately, changed the paths followed by the park's rivers. (To ecologists, this phenomenon is known as a "trophic cascade").

This is an example of complex entanglement. One part of a large system influences a completely different part of the system through a highly dynamic chain reaction. Few would have guessed that the introduction of wolves into a national park would alter the paths of rivers and the region's physical geography.

This example comes from a short documentary released in 2014 called *How Wolves Change Rivers.*[8] The video shows how scale, interdependence, and dynamism go hand in hand, and often produce unintended consequences. In the case of the gray wolves, the consequences of their reintroduction, while unintended, were not negative—they were part of a natural progression. But in an organization, unintended consequences can have decidedly negative impacts—on morale, on stakeholder relationships, on profitability, and so forth.

Unintended consequences are often the bane of transformation programs and a major contributor to the widely held belief among executives that most such programs fail. One executive told us that when he became the leader of a large organization, he received a real education in the unintended consequences and "black swans" that come with entanglement: "You wouldn't think that making a simple change, pulling this lever here, would make 10 other things explode behind me."

This phenomenon is sometimes referred to as the Cobra Effect. The term originated in the British Raj in 19th century India. The British government, concerned about the proliferation of venomous cobras in Delhi, offered a bounty to citizens who killed the snakes. Unfortunately, local residents reacted to this incentive by modifying their behavior in an unanticipated way: they began breeding cobras that could be killed

Getting our heads around the scale, interdependence, and dynamism of companies' organizational environments, and how we deliver transformation in this context, is a tall order, especially with our conventional technology and conceptual tools. This is the essence of the transformation dilemma confronting practitioners.

for money. When the government realized that citizens were gaming the system, they shut down the bounty program. This prompted the citizens to free their now-worthless snakes, significantly increasing the cobra population.

The level of complexity of entangled systems, the unforeseen feedback loops, blowback, and knock-on effects, even for relatively small or self-contained systems, can be very high. It's not surprising, therefore, that one key application of the world's most powerful supercomputers is modeling entangled natural systems such as the human body and weather patterns. An example is the use of the IBM Blue Gene/P computer to model 1 percent of the human brain, which comprises roughly 100 billion neurons and 100 *trillion* synapses (connections between neurons). Similarly, the US National Oceanic and Atmospheric Administration uses supercomputers to process vast amounts of data to model weather systems and climate change.

The systems represented by large organizations are not as complex as the human brain or global climate patterns. However, they are vastly more complex than executives and managers usually allow when designing and executing transformation programs.

Large and midsized incumbents spend millions (sometimes billions) of dollars on IT resources. Yet, while brain doctors and climatologists use cutting-edge supercomputers to model entangled systems, executives in most big companies use...Microsoft PowerPoint! This makes no sense and reflects the cramped way in which we generally think about how organizational systems work and how they can be changed.

Getting our heads around the scale, interdependence, and dynamism of companies' organizational environments, and how we deliver transformation in this context, is a tall order, especially with our conventional technology and conceptual tools.

This is the essence of the transformation dilemma confronting practitioners.

The theater of war offers a good example of how paralyzing this situation can be. Figure 8 depicts the complex entanglement that faced American commanders in Afghanistan, where multiple variables created a bewildering thicket of relationships, causes, and effects. US General Stanley A. McChrystal put the problem concisely after seeing this model in PowerPoint: "When we understand that slide, we'll have won the war."

Fig. 8: Military Entanglement in Afghanistan

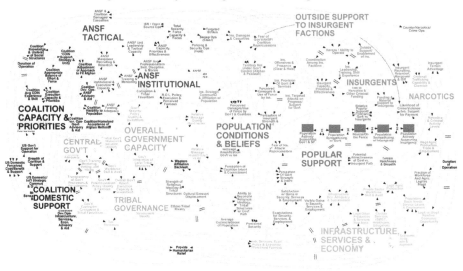

Source: PA Consulting, 2009

GETTING IN THE ZONE

What does all this add up to? And how is it any different from change challenges that organizations have faced for decades? (By some estimates, there are more than 80,000 book titles on Amazon.com falling under the topic of "change management."[9])

In our view, the sheer scope and scale of change associated with digital business transformation means that change management as a discipline must also transform. It must evolve to handle the entangled realities of scale, interdependence, and dynamism found in today's incumbents.

This level of entanglement is not merely high—it's growing. Figure 9 shows that a large majority of executives believe all three factors (scale, interdependence, and dynamism) have increased somewhat or significantly within their companies over the past five years.

Fig. 9: **Entanglement Is Getting Worse**

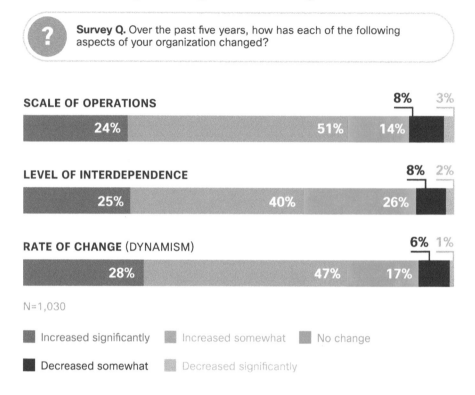

Survey Q. Over the past five years, how has each of the following aspects of your organization changed?

SCALE OF OPERATIONS — 8% · 3%

24% · 51% · 14%

LEVEL OF INTERDEPENDENCE — 8% · 2%

25% · 40% · 26%

RATE OF CHANGE (DYNAMISM) — 6% · 1%

28% · 47% · 17%

N=1,030

■ Increased significantly   ■ Increased somewhat   ■ No change
■ Decreased somewhat   ■ Decreased significantly

Source: Global Center for Digital Business Transformation, 2019

These findings underscore our point that the level of disorder (entropy) in organizations never decreases, just as in the physical universe of matter and space. In the corporate world, this is because of something called the "law of requisite variety," which organizational design theorist Jay Galbraith describes like this: "This law...states that as the number and variety of relevant entities in the stakeholder environment increases, the number and variety of units inside the enterprise must increase in order to manage these entities."[10]

As our economies shift from mass production to mass *customization* for customers, we have many more products, many more market segments, many more partners, and many more sales teams. Many more ways of doing everything. This requires "the creation of more—and more sophisticated—integrating mechanisms."[11]

In addition, changes in business models, how companies create value for customers, and how often they need to change the way they operate, all suggest that the *extent* of transformation is also new. In some cases, the change is truly existential. As Andy Weir, CIO at Bankwest of Australia, declared, "Rather than think like a bank that is slowly increasing its digital capabilities, we're thinking about ourselves as a digital organization that provides financial services. Specifically, in how we organize ourselves to build and create amazing customer experiences."

And in almost every case, the need for change never ends. It's perpetual. As Alan Stukalsky, CDO of $5 billion HR solutions and services provider Randstad North America, explained in our interview, "Our transformation has been five years, so it obviously hasn't been easy. And it's still going. It's not something that's ever going to have a 'We're done!' flag."

In sum, companies need a more nuanced view of organizational change. In Figure 10, we divide the change challenge into the *context of transformation* and the *extent of transformation* to create two different zones that help to classify change efforts.

Fig. 10: **Change Management vs. Orchestration**

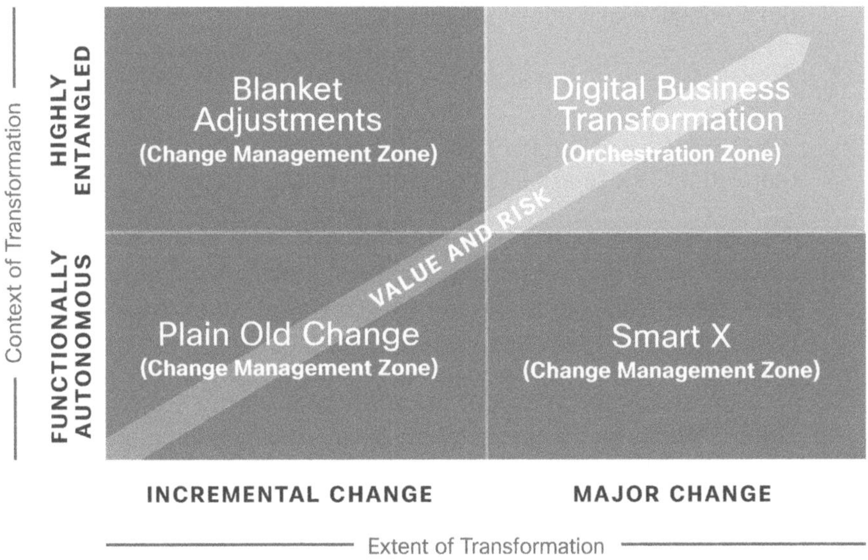

	INCREMENTAL CHANGE	MAJOR CHANGE
HIGHLY ENTANGLED	Blanket Adjustments (Change Management Zone)	Digital Business Transformation (Orchestration Zone)
FUNCTIONALLY AUTONOMOUS	Plain Old Change (Change Management Zone)	Smart X (Change Management Zone)

Context of Transformation (vertical axis) — *Extent of Transformation* (horizontal axis) — VALUE AND RISK

Source: Global Center for Digital Business Transformation, 2019

There are four types of change:

1. **Plain Old Change.** This is functionally autonomous, incremental change. The goal of change is straightforward, and the resources needed are limited and well-defined within a particular functional area or group. For example, if the advertising department opts to shift investment in newspaper and television media to online ads, that's their purview. It doesn't significantly impact, and isn't contingent upon, other parts of the company.

    This type of change represents most of the management effort focused on implementing changes. It's pretty run-of-the-mill and doesn't involve extensive cross-functional considerations. It also doesn't require changes to a company's overarching strategy or business model.

2. **Blanket Adjustments.** This is highly entangled, incremental change. Here, a company makes a tweak or calibration—introducing new enterprise-wide hiring rules or a global expense management system—that affects many different stakeholders in all parts of the organization. These adjustments frequently collide with highly entangled structures and, as many of us have experienced, can be challenging to implement. Nonetheless, the extent of change isn't large. There's no essential change to the kinds of value the company creates for customers, how it makes money, or its overall competitive position.

3. **Smart X.** This is functionally autonomous, major change. The changes are big, but they don't have a company-wide focus. When you hear about projects like "smart supply chain" or "smart real estate," these are examples of Smart X change.

    This doesn't mean, however, that Smart X change is a breeze to achieve. Although the change may be limited to a single function, it can be ambitious in scope. A "smart factory," for example, could involve a complete revolution in how manufacturing processes are performed. This certainly qualifies as "major change."

4. **Digital Business Transformation.** This is highly entangled, major change. This type of change is the focus of the DBT Center in general and this book in particular. Recalling our earlier definition of digital business transformation as "organizational change through the use of digital technologies and business models to

improve performance," we can see that this type of change is considerably different from the others.

It combines high levels of scale, interdependence, and dynamism with the need to make fundamental changes to the entire organization in the service of a new strategic direction. It means making changes to business models and customer value creation to address disruptive competition. It may also involve value creation with third parties (i.e., through platforms).

As organizations move "upward" in the framework, the level of entanglement increases. As they move "to the right," both the scope and difficulty of change increase. And when they move "upward *and* to the right," the potential payoff (value) gets bigger, while risk, and the need for orchestration, intensifies.

Many organizations are pursuing change in multiple quadrants at the same time, as shown in Figure 11. A sizable minority (34 percent) are working in the top right quadrant, on what we define as digital business transformation, as part of their portfolio of change activities.

Fig. 11: **Most Organizations Are Pursuing Multiple Types of Change at Once**

Survey Q. Which of the following types of changes or transformations is your organization currently undertaking?

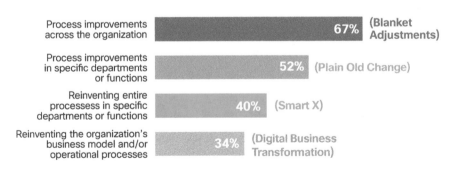

Process improvements across the organization	67% (Blanket Adjustments)
Process improvements in specific departments or functions	52% (Plain Old Change)
Reinventing entire processess in specific departments or functions	40% (Smart X)
Reinventing the organization's business model and/or operational processes	34% (Digital Business Transformation)

N=1,030

Source: Global Center for Digital Business Transformation, 2019

"A lot of companies think they are doing digital transformation, but they are actually only doing basic digitization or digital 'optimization' without addressing the core fundamental problems: culture, leadership, operating model, talent, funding," said Ibrahim Gokcen, former CDO of $31 billion Danish shipping and container logistics giant A.P. Moller-Maersk. Digital business transformation then is the really big stuff, highly strategic, done at scale, and with a holistic focus.

Many change efforts are touted as being "end-to-end" in nature. In reality, though, most tend to address the types of change represented in the first three quadrants. Because these three are fairly amenable to traditional change management approaches, they fall into what we call the "Change Management Zone" (shown in blue in Figure 10), where planning and standardization are staples. (Some of those 80,000 volumes on Amazon.com about change management may help here.)

But change management programs fall short when it comes to the fourth type of change, digital business transformation. Why? Because they take a highly linear approach to a task that is exponential in nature.

John Kotter has become a godfather of change management (and rightly so), but it's telling that his best-known framework for organizational change is an "eight-stage process" that is distinctly linear in nature[12] (see Figure 12). Precisely because digital business transformation involves making big changes across *multiple* aspects of the business, conventional change management is ill-suited to fostering major changes in highly entangled organizations.

Fig. 12: Kotter's Eight Stages of Change Management

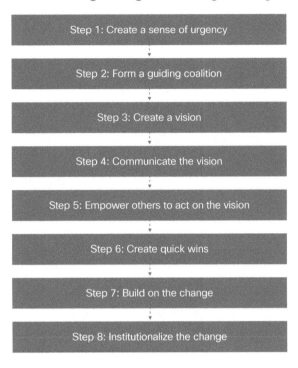

Step 1: Create a sense of urgency

Step 2: Form a guiding coalition

Step 3: Create a vision

Step 4: Communicate the vision

Step 5: Empower others to act on the vision

Step 6: Create quick wins

Step 7: Build on the change

Step 8: Institutionalize the change

Source: Adapted from John Kotter, Leading Change, 1996

The consistent focus of firms on isolated change efforts, rather than on more expansive enterprise-wide change, is both a cause and a symptom of the reliance on traditional change-management regimens like the widely used Prosci ADKAR model and others.[13] As historically conceived, change management is more appropriate when the context of change is straightforward and the extent is limited. However, even within these parameters, most organizational change fails. This isn't to say that tried-and-true precepts like the establishment of a "burning platform" or a "guiding coalition" are wrong. But most big organizations don't have the necessary under-

Orchestrate | verb | *[awr-kuh-streyt]*

To mobilize and enable so as to achieve a desired effect.

standing or agility (more on this later) to pull off a large-scale change in a manner that reflects the exigencies of the Digital Vortex.

To do that, companies need to move beyond classical change management to a different realm, the **Orchestration Zone** (shown in green in Figure 10), that can handle the networked nature of organizations and the unprecedented extent of change required. In the Orchestration Zone, companies can drive change in a way that is organizationally transverse, creating business outcomes on multiple fronts, and allowing them to transform again and again and again. Operating in the Orchestration Zone means taking a highly connected approach to change.

THE POWER OF ORCHESTRATION

What does it mean to "orchestrate"? The DBT Center's definition is "to mobilize and enable so as to achieve a desired effect."

Orchestration is a topic that has come up only occasionally in the management literature, although this is changing, at least in terms of vocabulary, if not in actionable guidance.[14] To date, the study of orchestration in a management context has focused primarily outside the four walls of the business—often at the "edge," where value chains, strategic alliances, and platforms come into play.

Hong Kong-based supply chain giant Li & Fung is one of the best-known examples of a company deemed to have an "orchestrator" business model—one based on connecting players across the value chain.[15] Selling primarily to American and European consumer brands and retailers, its core competency has become the orchestration of suppliers. This approach has enabled Li & Fung to profitably generate nearly $20 billion in annual revenue from apparel, furniture, beauty and personal care products, and other fashion wares, without owning a factory. In fact, Li & Fung has no manufacturing capabilities whatsoever.[16]

Li & Fung can mobilize a global supply chain linking 8,000 customers and 15,000 suppliers because it operates as a networked organization.[17] The value in its business model is the ability to connect customers to the right network of suppliers to orchestrate materials sourcing, production, storage, and the movement of goods. The company sources raw materials like yarn, dyes, fabrics, and furniture elements; coordinates manufacturing with thousands of factories around the world; and manages the shipping and logistics services for components and end products. Li & Fung can quickly and flexibly change a source if risks arise or disruptions occur.

Another example of orchestration comes from the world of open innovation. Here, the focus is on capitalizing on ideas from people who don't work for you, using an ecosystem, platform, or network of some kind. Organizations such as IDEO and the Stanford d.school, and authors like Henry Chesbrough and Don Tapscott, have helped convert the idea of open innovation into a veritable industry in its own right. In parallel, a horde of consultancies, interactive agencies, and incubators has sprung up to help companies orchestrate ideas from third parties and create better, faster innovation.

LEGO, the $5 billion Danish toy maker, offers a well-known example of how a company can orchestrate open innovation. Since the 1950s, the firm has been a household name for children and parents worldwide thanks to its modular plastic bricks that allow customers to imagine and build all manner of creations.

In 1998 LEGO launched a new toy offer, a robotic kit called LEGO Mindstorms. Months after the launch, the software operating the robots was "reverse-engineered" and communities of users building new capabilities flourished. After some hesitation and initial focus on protecting their intellectual property, LEGO's leadership fully embraced and facilitated these vibrant communities of fans and users. Today, the LEGO IDEAS page enables consumers to submit their proposals for new forms of LEGO toys, contests, and events, making third-party orchestration not just an experiment for the company, but a mainstay of its business.[18]

But orchestration is not purely an external concept. What if we considered how ecosystems, platforms, and networks could be brought to bear on a company's *internal* change effort? Our research tells us that companies must extend orchestration beyond familiar domains like supply chain or open innovation, and apply it to digital business transformation.

When it comes to transformation, organizations face a thorny dilemma grounded in three conjoined issues: scale, interdependence, and dynamism. The responses to this dilemma of entanglement are both classic and flawed.

If you're an organizational change practitioner, one who wants to drive strategic change at scale, you can try planning or standardization (Thompson's prescribed approaches for sequential and pooled interdependence). You can also try departmentalization or running some digital pilots.

These approaches seek simplicity. But simplification is only a small part of executing a digital business transformation. Planning, standardization, departmentalization, and pilots have their place in the change portfolio, but when it comes to major change in highly entangled organizations, they just don't cut it.

Transformation orthodoxies grounded in linear thinking are truly resources for yesterday, not playbooks for life in the Digital Vortex. As we like to say, "Straight lines are straitjackets." The organizational characteristics we've described present a monumental task for transformation leaders because they challenge the limits of typical managerial decision-making. For decades, executives have made linear concepts, tools, and mental models their go-to's when it comes time to change the business. Think about how budgets work, or waterfall development in IT, or the flowcharts of the project management world, or for that matter, any proposal you've ever seen from a management consultancy. All of these approaches fail to account for the entangled nature of organizations.

CHAPTER 2
Understanding Guiding Objectives

FIRE, READY, AIM

In our workshops, we often separate executives into teams, giving each group a puzzle to solve. They look like regular jigsaw puzzles, but there's a twist: they cannot be solved using normal approaches.

For example, each piece has a shiny painted side and an unpainted wood side. The solution requires mixing the painted and unpainted sides together. And, among other things, the "corner pieces" do not go in the corners.

After we give the executives minimal instructions ("You have 10 minutes to solve the puzzle. Go!"), they jump straight into execution mode. Wearing agitated expressions, they typically start by turning over all the pieces so that the painted sides face upward. Then, they start "solving" the puzzle.

This never works.

After a while, someone will tentatively turn over a piece to reveal the ugly unpainted side. The rest of the group usually regards this action with disdain. "Stop playing around!" another team member might say. "We're running out of time." The first teammate then turns the piece back over, painted side up.

They rarely finish the puzzle in the allotted time. The puzzle isn't difficult to solve. Someone who has never seen a puzzle could probably solve it in a few minutes. The problem for the executives is twofold. First, they become slaves to their assumptions about puzzles—shiny sides should face upward, and pieces with right angles need to go in the corners. Second, from the very start, they don't take time to truly understand the challenge.

If they did, they might ask, "Why is the instructor asking us to solve a puzzle?" or "What's different about this puzzle?" or "What should the finished puzzle look like?"

In other words, they would spend more time thinking about the *problem,* rather than executing a *solution.*

The same is true for digital business transformation. In fact, one CDO we interviewed described his company's transformation as "a million-piece jigsaw puzzle where no one is sure what the picture is supposed to look like." How can you possibly begin to execute when that's the case?

Before jumping straight into execution, organizations need to understand the opportunities and threats they're facing. But like the executives with the puzzle, too many transformation programs follow a "fire, ready, aim" approach. There is a strong (and understandable) desire to get on with the change, to drive results. As such, many change efforts are like cars that rev their engines to the maximum RPM but remain stuck in neutral. A lot of resources are consumed, but there's no movement.

As Sun Tzu maintained in *The Art of War,* strategy without execution is the slowest route to victory; execution without strategy is the noise before defeat. In a recent *Harvard Business Review* article, our IMD colleagues Anand Narasimhan and Jean-Louis Barsoux put their fingers on the issue of placing the execution cart before the horse of strategic direction:

> Studies consistently report that about three-quarters of change efforts flop—either they fail to deliver the anticipated benefits or they are abandoned entirely. Because flawed implementation is most often blamed for such failures, organizations have focused on improving execution.... But poor execution is only part of the problem; our analysis suggests that misdiagnosis is equally to blame. Often organizations pursue the wrong changes—especially in complex and fast-moving environments, where decisions about what to transform in order to remain competitive can be hasty or misguided.[1]

Together, the organizational entanglement we described in the last chapter and the volatile dynamics of the Digital Vortex are the very embodiment of the "complex and fast-moving environments" the authors cite. Many transformation efforts are doomed before they even start, due to a lack of clarity about where the "goal posts" are. As American sports icon Yogi Berra once said, "If you don't know where you're going, you'll end up someplace else."

In truth, many transformation programs are a loose confederacy of vague intentions, skunkworks projects, and "random acts of enablement," as one practitioner put it. They are a transformation smorgasbord where everyone defines the work and how it should be done to suit their own tastes.

What's more, too many transformations are disconnected from the customer value creation, business models, and strategies of the company. We refer to these three elements together as **guiding objectives.** Guiding objectives are a set of clearly-articulated aims that serve as the point of departure for effective execution of a transformation program. (However, they are not the company's "digital strategy"; see sidebar.)

Guiding objectives must be set at the *line of business* level. An organization may have dozens of business lines, each facing different opportunities and threats. In the case of a business school like IMD, they may include an MBA program, an executive MBA program, open enrollment programs, customized programs for individual companies, online programs, and so on. Business lines might also include product categories or markets.

Forget Digital for a Second

We are often asked how to build a digital strategy. This is the wrong question, at least if what you really want to accomplish is an organizational transformation.

As one CDO we interviewed noted, "If a 'digital' initiative is not an extension of a priority the business has established, it's meaningless. Defining a 'digital' strategy is a dead end."

We define "digital" as "the convergence of multiple technology innovations enabled by connectivity." This includes all kinds of technologies such as cloud computing, analytics, the Internet of Things (IoT), mobility, social media, and a lot more.

Digital tools and technologies are relevant to strategy, but they do not deserve a strategy of their own. Does it really make sense to have an organizational strategy *and* a digital strategy? What if they conflict?

(Continued on next page)

Forget Digital for a Second

(Continued from previous page)

"Strategy" itself is too narrow a construct to drive execution. Properly understood, digital is an enabler of strategy, which is itself one element of guiding objectives.

As we'll demonstrate, a company's approaches to customer value creation (and the business models on which it depends) also play a key role.

As we make clear, "digital" and "transformation" are not the same thing. "Digital transformation is much more about people, and culture, and attitudes, and the way you live your life, over what technologies you are using," said Firdaus Bhathena, CDO at Aetna, one of America's leading diversified health care benefits companies. "The whole point of a digital transformation is that you make it part of your DNA, to be the best in the world at leveraging technology for your business."

Setting uniform guiding objectives for customer value creation, business model, and strategy across a multi-line business makes little sense and is unlikely to yield executable results.

CUSTOMER VALUE CREATION AND BUSINESS MODELS

How should companies think about guiding objectives? To answer this, let's revisit some key concepts from *Digital Vortex*. (For those who have read the earlier book, this chapter will serve as a quick refresher; Chapter 3 will explain how to establish guiding objectives for your company's businesses, and how these concepts set the stage for executing a transformation program.)

The first element of guiding objectives is the organization's approach to *customer value creation*. This must be foremost in the minds of leaders. They must crisply define "what's in it for the customer." Lots of people talk about putting the customer first, but this is honored more in the breach than in the observance. When it comes to transforming successfully, however, customer value creation is an absolute necessity.

At the core of disruption is the creation of new and better forms of value. This value does not take the form of revenues or profits, but of value for end customers. Quite simply, disruptors create market change by figuring out a way to provide better customer value.

While preparing to write *Digital Vortex,* we studied more than 100 of the most successful disruptors to find common denominators in their *modus operandi.* We found three (shown in Figure 13). Disruptors create value for customers through lower costs or by creating some kind of economic gain (cost value); through customer experiences that are faster, more convenient, more personalized, and so forth (experience value); and by creating connections that did not exist before, such as between a buyer and a seller, or between a teacher and a student (platform value).

Fig. 13: Three Forms of Customer Value

Cost Value   Experience Value   Platform Value

Source: Global Center for Digital Business Transformation, 2015-2019

COST VALUE

Cost value is created when a disruptor offers a product or service that is significantly cheaper than existing alternatives. The extreme example is a free alternative to a paid-for product or service—for example, Skype or WhatsApp. Disruptors may also create cost value by dematerializing physical products such as books, music, and videos. Conferencing software providers create cost value by reducing the need for business travel, for example.

Cost value is often the first target of disruptors, and it's also the hardest to maintain. Other disruptors can match lower prices (it didn't take long for imitators to match Skype's offer of free communication), and incumbents can reduce their own prices. Uber began as a cheap alternative to taxis, but if this were its only benefit, it would probably not have survived.

EXPERIENCE VALUE

Uber's popularity grew not only because it was cheaper than taxis, but because it was better in other ways. Uber vehicles were easier to hail (through an app), they were perceived as safer, and payment was easier. These and other benefits were not linked to the price, but to the customer experience. Hence, the second form of customer value is *experience value*.

Experience value can create a variety of benefits, such as more convenience or higher quality. As with cost value, experience value increases as offerings are digitized. What was once physical and indivisible can now be partitioned into only those elements that customers want, and then delivered instantly to any device or location. The superior experiences offered by disruptors can make it hard for incumbents to maintain market share based on brand or quality. With digital, it's also easy for customers to move their business to a new provider.

Although the competitive advantages of experience value are easier to sustain than those of cost value, they *can* be copied. Other disruptors—such as Lyft or Grab Taxi—can imitate Uber's model, and traditional taxi companies can introduce Uber-like service improvements. To build a sustainable model, Uber turned to a third category of value.

PLATFORM VALUE

Uber's appeal was not limited to price (cost value) and quality of service (experience value). There was also value in its scale. For the frequent traveler, for example, the fact that Uber's app worked the same way in most parts of the world had enormous utility. Moreover, because the company acquired information on millions of customers, it could extend the platform to other domains—such as food delivery (Uber Eats) and shipping (Uber Freight). Uber's platform also amounted to what is known as a "multi-sided" market—it's a market for drivers too, not just for passengers. The connections between both sides of the market benefited its users in new and compelling ways. This is *platform value*.

Platform value disrupts competition by introducing an exponential element. Platforms create network effects—situations in which the number or type of users impacts the value that they receive. More users mean more value for users.

Once they're successfully established, the networked nature of platforms makes them harder to dislodge. This can lead to "winner-takes-all" effects in which dominant platform owners disproportionately realize the gains. This logic is the basis of many of the most dynamic and game-changing digital business models, including those of Facebook, Google, Amazon, Spotify, Fortnite publisher Epic Games, and, of course, Uber.

COMBINATORIAL DISRUPTION

Successful disruptors rarely create only one type of value for their customers. Indeed, it's very difficult to become a long-term disruptor this way. The strongest disruptors are proficient at blending innovative products and services to create customer value in a way that deepens market disruption. In our earlier book, we called this situation, in which a company creates all three forms of value simultaneously, *combinatorial disruption.*

Combinatorial disruption illustrates how customer value can be created, combined, and leveraged to crush traditional business models. However, few companies ever deliver the combinatorial disruption "triple threat" of cost value, experience value, and platform value.

In the past, as described in Michael Porter's classic *Competitive Strategy,* firms focused on one of two main competitive orientations: cost leadership (what we refer to as "cost value") and differentiation (what we call "experience value").[2] Porter's point is that companies pick one or the other: you can be Walmart (cost value) or you can be Burberry (experience value). But you don't try to do both at once—doing so would be a recipe for disaster (by the way, there were not platforms as we think of them today back when Porter wrote his book). Companies like Uber, and all of the most disruptive companies, smash this paradigm with their ability to create combinatorial disruption that customers can't get enough of.

The next (related) element in guiding objectives is *business models.* Following Alexander Osterwalder and Yves Pigneur, authors of *Busi-*

ness Model Generation, and architects of the well-known "Business Model Canvas," we hold that "a business model describes the rationale of how an organization creates, delivers, and captures value."[3] Business models put customer value creation into operation.[i] They dictate how products, channels, operations and so forth are used to create, deliver, and capture value.

DBT Center research revealed that disruptors create market change by harnessing 15 types of business models[ii] to enable the creation, delivery, and capture of the three forms of customer value described above (see Figure 14).

Fig. 14: Categorization of Disruptive Business Models

Cost Value	Experience Value	Platform Value
Free / ultra-low cost	Customer empowerment	Ecosystem
Buyer aggregation	Customization	Crowdsourcing
Price transparency	Instant gratification	Communities
Reverse auctions	Reduced friction	Digital marketplaces
Consumption-based pricing	Automation	Data orchestrator

Source: Global Center for Digital Business Transformation, 2015-2019

STRATEGY

In *Digital Vortex,* we also identified two new competitive phenomena. The first is the bad news: a type of disruptive competitor we called the "value vampire." The defining characteristic of value vampires is that they permanently shrink the revenues or profits (or both) of the

---

i   For this reason, it's worth noting that the importance of business models as an element of a transformation's guiding objectives applies equally to public sector and nonprofit entities. Governments, universities, and non-governmental organizations all have customers for whom they must create value. For that matter, all the frameworks presented in this book can be applied in organizations that operate in the public sphere.

ii Space does not permit a discussion of these 15 business models here. For those interested in learning more, they are covered in detail in Chapter 2 of *Digital Vortex.* These business models are important not just because they are threat vectors for incumbents, but because they are tools incumbents can use to harness disruption for their own competitive gain.

markets they attack. Value vampires are dangerous for incumbents because they are ruthlessly efficient at creating customer value. They lure customers with cost value, reducing the revenue and profit within a market segment. With experience value, they make it attractive for customers to switch. With platform value, they create stickiness for their customers.

Disruptors differ sharply from incumbents not only because of their business models but because of how they operate and execute. For disruptive competitors, what matters is the "value, not the value chain." As a result, disruptors are "unbundling" entire industries and carving off incumbents' most profitable business segments. This is happening in banking, for example, where hundreds of "fintechs" are reinventing loans, mortgages, payments, wealth management, and more. They provide their services without physical branches and financial advisers. This lowers their distribution costs and eliminates middlemen and high-touch service models.

But digital disruption is not all bad news for incumbents. As industries move toward the center of the Digital Vortex, where digitization and disruption are most intense, "value vacancies" may also arise. These are the good news. A value vacancy is a market opportunity that can be profitably exploited via digital disruption. Companies can enjoy a period of fast growth, high margins, and a privileged market position. However, these periods are increasingly short. Established competitors from other industries, startups, and value vampires soon intrude. So companies must exploit a succession of value vacancies to maintain growth.

How do traditional companies respond to value vampires and other disruptors? How can they become disruptors themselves, wielding digital technologies and business models to create competitive advantage? In addition to creating cost value, experience value, and platform value in new ways, and a business model to operationalize this value creation, they need the third component of guiding objectives: strategy.

In *Digital Vortex,* we identified four strategies for doing this: Harvest, Retreat, Disrupt, and Occupy. We refer to these, collectively, as the *Strategic Response Playbook* (see Figure 15). The first two options (left side) are defensive strategies—they help to enhance or protect existing business lines. Defensive strategies are used to fend off value vampires, as well as more modest threats, and to maximize the useful lifespan of businesses under attack. The second two strategies (right side) are offensive. They help an organization compete with a disruptor directly or *become* the disruptor. Offensive strategies pursue new value.

Fig. 15: **Strategic Response Playbook**

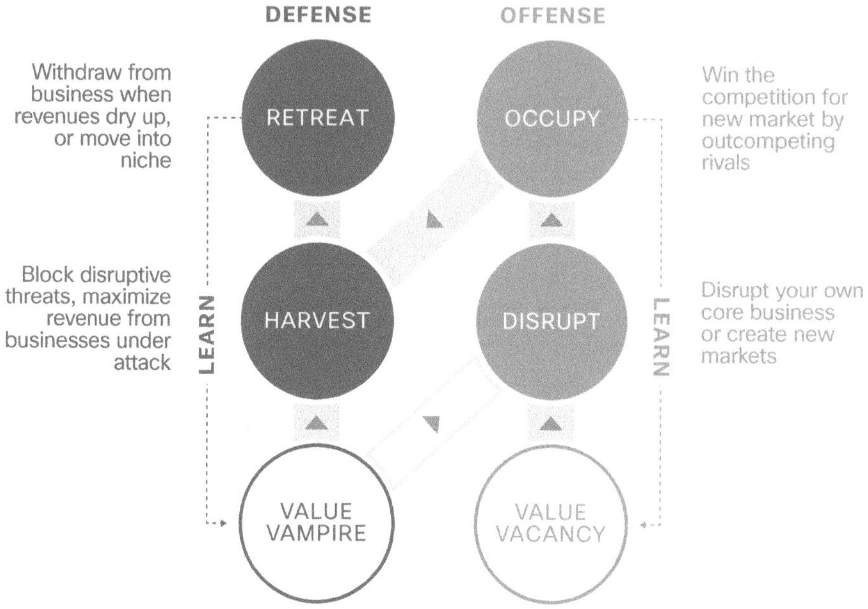

DEFENSE **OFFENSE**

Withdraw from business when revenues dry up, or move into niche

RETREAT OCCUPY

Win the competition for new market by outcompeting rivals

Block disruptive threats, maximize revenue from businesses under attack

LEARN HARVEST DISRUPT LEARN

Disrupt your own core business or create new markets

VALUE VAMPIRE

VALUE VACANCY

Source: Global Center for Digital Business Transformation, 2015-2019

Harvest: Maximizing Returns from a Disrupted Business

Harvest is a defensive strategy designed to maximize gains from an at-risk or declining business. Harvest strategies frequently begin with "blocking tactics," drawing on the benefits of incumbent status with customers, partners, regulators, opinion-makers, and providers of capital. These countermeasures are intended to slow the disruption or buy time for an incumbent to come up with a more appropriate response. Tactics may include legal action to halt disruptor operations, marketing activities to challenge disruptor claims, or the use of financial resources to undercut disruptor pricing. Rarely, however, do such blocking tactics foil the disruption entirely.

A Harvest strategy tries to make the best of a challenging situation by optimizing the margin that can be extracted during the period of decline. It involves significant organizational reconfiguration to adapt the business to the new reality. This may include a combination of the following steps: consolidation of operations; cost optimization and streamlining of processes; stepping down production; locking in loyal or dependent customer segments; emphasizing quality and brand equity in marketing; and pruning portfolio elements that no longer contribute enough to value creation.

Harvest shouldn't be equated with failure. It's the natural progression of a mature business confronting commoditization, customer attrition, margin compression, and other unpleasantness arising from digital disruption. Leaders who are clear-sighted enough to accept this are best positioned to steer their organizations through the transition.

An example of a global incumbent adopting a Harvest strategy is Avon Products.[4] Founded over 130 years ago in New York, the company uses a direct, social-selling channel: 6 million "Avon Ladies" form an independent salesforce of micro-entrepreneurs who go door-to-door to offer women cosmetics, fragrances, jewelry, and health supplements.

But with rapid consumer adoption of digital retail channels, savvy new competitors like Walmart, Ulta Beauty, and Sephora have swooped in, offering affordable cosmetics and improving the consumer experience, both online and in retail stores.[5] Avon's revenue was nearly halved from peak sales of $11.3 billion in 2011 to $5.7 billion in 2017.[6] Profits flat-lined and and stayed low.[7] The company's stock cratered.

Jan Zijderveld, Avon Products' new CEO, is realistic about this disruption: "Avon is operating in a dramatically changing consumer and competitive environment and business as usual is not an option... We're taking a fresh look at everything, with a sense of urgency that you would expect. There are no quick fixes."[8]

With a new leadership team, Avon has made operational moderniza-
tion through digitization its main priority.[9] The company is keeping its
major strength—direct personal engagement with sales representatives and end customers—while making comprehensive improvements
across many areas of its operating model via digital-enabled capabilities. Among other things, it has focused investment in emerging
markets and groomed a next generation of representatives. As the
Financial Times noted, "The most common Avon Lady in 2017 is not
the 1950s American housewife, but rather millennial women selling
mascara in Rio or Manila through YouTube."[10]

For Avon, a Harvest strategy has meant rejuvenating the brand with
provocative marketing campaigns that target millennials; expanding
its social media presence; reducing the time to bring new offers to
market from two years to a few months; training and providing mobile
productivity tools to sales representatives; revisiting incentive compensation to retain sellers; using analytics to better target and serve
customers; and reducing operating costs by standardizing its digital
infrastructure. By lowering costs and improving the experience for
sellers and customers, Avon's Harvest strategy has helped it cope
with aggressive new forms of disruptive competition.

Since 2016, the company's revenue has stabilized. In 2017, it returned to profitability and positive cash flow from operations for the
first time since 2011.

Retreat: Strategic Withdrawal

Harvest is about improving customer experiences and operational efficiency in threatened segments. But when the costs of maintaining
a business outstrip the benefits, companies should focus on *Retreat.*

There are two main components to a Retreat strategy. First, Retreat
emphasizes withdrawal into a market niche that serves a small subset
of existing customers with specialized needs. Usually, the niche is a
market the incumbent has dominated in the past and, in most cases,
is an expert at managing for profitability. The niche market often requires a level of experience value that is hard for disruptors to deliver.
Thus, a Retreat strategy is largely about increasing specialized expe-

rience value within a niche to such an extent that disruptors find it very difficult to compete or consider that niche not worth their time.

Fujifilm provides an excellent example of a Retreat strategy. On January 14, 2012, *The Economist* published a story titled, "Kodak Is at Death's Door; Fujifilm, Its Old Rival, Is Thriving. Why?"[11] Like Kodak, which declared bankruptcy a few days after that story appeared, Fujifilm recognized the digital threat to its core market in analog cameras and film. As far back as the 1980s, both companies anticipated declining sales of photographic film and paper and launched successful digital camera offerings. By 1999, Fujifilm was the world leader in digital camera sales.

By 2003, however, the disruption in digital photography deepened with the introduction of smartphones with built-in multi-megapixel cameras. At Fujifilm, film sales fell off a cliff. They dropped by one-third within a year, and photo labs reported an 80 percent decline in processing jobs for consumers.

After decades of growth, Fujifilm's revenue reached a peak in 1999 at $13.6 billion. Shigetaka Komori, who became CEO in 2003 (he was also named chairman in 2012), had to respond: "At first I thought that color film wouldn't disappear quickly, but digital stole it all away in an instant." This is a common sentiment for executives who have the misfortune of encountering value vampires—disruptive competitors who permanently undercut the viability of a market.

In 2001, film accounted for two-thirds of Fujifilm profits. By 2017, it was less than 1 percent.[12]

Komori and his team restructured the organization, reducing its distribution, research and development, and management costs. Significant job reductions, factory closings, and other cuts helped decrease the company's cost base by more than $5 billion.

Fujifilm diversified and retreated into a few niche markets where value vampires (Apple and the Android-based smartphone makers) had no intention of following: high-end digital imaging machines, enterprise document solutions, and (unexpectedly) cosmetics.[13]

Human skin, like photographs, deteriorates with age due to oxidation caused by exposure to ultraviolet rays. Therefore, it was a sensible move for Fujifilm to leverage its know-how in anti-oxidation technology and chemistry to help fight wrinkles. Fujifilm's advanced skincare products, sold under the brand ASTALIFT, are thriving.[14] Today, cosmetics and pharmaceuticals (another new market) are the company's most profitable divisions, delivering more than $3.4 billion in sales in 2017.[15]

Market exit is the second component of a Retreat strategy, and choosing the right time to exit is a critical decision. Too early, and you risk leaving money on the table. Too late, and the value has disappeared. Fujifilm sold many of its core assets in film and paper production while they still had value, channeling the proceeds into new business lines.

As with Harvest, Retreat strategies are not a sign of failure. In fact, they can allow a company to exploit new opportunities that will replace diminishing revenue streams with business lines where ROI is stronger. Indeed, Fujifilm's overall 2018 revenue, in excess of $21.6 billion, is two-thirds higher than in 1999.

Retreat strategies are different from Harvesting because they mostly involve "wrapping up" the core business, rather than devoting resources and energy to "wringing out" the remaining value. With Retreat, the market opportunity has been exhausted, and only a niche profit pool remains.

Let's pause for a moment to consider what the two defensive strategies, Harvest and Retreat, mean in terms of executing organizational change. In some cases, these strategies may involve significant—even painful—change, such as restructuring, sunsetting, or selling off a once-lucrative line of business.

But using the 2x2 framework in Figure 10, we can say that most Harvest and Retreat efforts do not fall into the top right quadrant, the Orchestration Zone. The changes associated with Harvest and Retreat are quite amenable to the more standard approaches in the Change Management Zone. These strategies are often relatively limited in scope, involving just one or two parts of the business. Hence, they don't require major changes to the business model. If the line of business in question were a car, Harvest and Retreat strategies would imply offering the car to consumers at a lower cost and with some specialized features, or perhaps exiting this segment of the market.

What if the company that sells this car also wants to enter an adjacent high-growth digital business—for example, by providing value-added navigation services to other manufacturers? To do that, we need to look at the right side of the Strategic Response Playbook, where companies go on offense.

Disrupt: Creating New Customer Value

A Disrupt strategy focuses on creating cost value, experience value, and platform value for customers using digital technologies and business models in a new way. Becoming a disruptor requires a mix of deep customer and competitor insights, innovative thinking, strategic experimentation, capability transfer and building, and careful investment.

As a result, many incumbents find disruption very difficult. As Clayton Christensen observed, "The reason it is so difficult for existing firms to capitalize on disruptive innovations is that their processes and their business model, [which] make them good at the existing business, actually make them bad at competing for the disruption."[16] Too many companies focus only on their current value chains rather than alternatives that would better solve customer problems. And creating a better solution to customer problems is the essence of market disruption.

In a fragmented and increasingly competitive mattress industry, two online leaders—Casper,[17] a startup founded in 2014 in the United States, and Endy,[18] launched in 2015 in Canada—provide excellent examples of Disrupt strategies.

Global mattress and mattress component sales are growing at a healthy 6 to 7 percent annually, and are expected to exceed $80 billion over the next decade.[19] In North America, many factors are driving sales increases that outpace population growth[20]: improvements in mattress products, an aging population driving more demand for housing and associated products, growth in the hospitality industry, an increased focus on health and wellness, growing awareness of the health consequences of sleep disorders, and a greater consciousness about environmental sustainability among millennials.[21] This opportunity is attracting venture capital investment into more than 100 startups targeting the mattress market,[22] as well as competition from digital giants like Amazon.[23]

Casper and Endy's success is the result of their rigorous focus on providing value to customers. Buying a mattress through traditional channels can be a painful experience. Difficulty in comparing prices across brands, high retail margins, abusive sales tactics, a long and cumbersome delivery process, and consumer confusion with the diversity of offers all contribute to buyer frustration.

Although 90 percent of mattress sales still occur in retail stores, where customers can try the products, preferences are changing fast.[24] Casper and Endy were among the first companies to offer mattresses online. They carefully researched how they could address concerns, continuously innovated to offer a premium sleep experience,[25] and educated and engaged customers in fun new ways.[26]

They offer affordable products, free delivery, extended trial periods, and free returns. By compressing and folding mattresses into boxes the size of a file cabinet, they are also making deliveries easier. And, unlike many 1990s startups that sold mattresses by phone, Casper and Endy design and manufacture their own products. They create materials that take sleep patterns into account, provide better comfort and support, relieve pressure points, and release body heat faster.[27]

As some of their innovations become "table stakes," these two disruptors keep innovating to stay ahead of the competition. Casper recently announced that it's expanding into bedding accessories, with new sheet and pillow designs. It is also building a physical retail presence to complement its e-commerce channel. In addition, it recently announced an alliance with mass merchandise leader Target,[28] is opening pop-up stores at Nordstrom,[29] and has created a flagship lounge called Dreamery in Manhattan.[30]

As they gain market share and popularity, the two companies are forc-ing consolidation among incumbent competitors.[31] In October 2018, the largest mattress chain in the United States, Mattress Firm, with some 3,300 stores, filed for bankruptcy.[32]

Occupy: Winning in a Disrupted Space

Where Disrupt strategies introduce market disruption, Occupy strat-egies focus on *sustaining* the competitive gains associated with dis-ruption. As with Harvesting and Disrupting, incumbents sometimes struggle with Occupy strategies. When people speak about the chal-lenges incumbents face in "becoming disruptors," they're often refer-ring to their inability to succeed with Occupy strategies. And as the value vacancy matures or the new market is itself disrupted, com-panies must shift from an offensive footing (Occupy) to a defensive Harvest strategy to maximize revenue and profits.

The main problem with Occupy is that incumbents are often on unfa-miliar terrain. Disruption can be born of market adjacencies, new mar-ket creation, or digital enhancements to existing markets. In all three cases, the incumbent is operating in new territory. It's a land where managers have no rules of the road, no tried-and-true approaches, and no coping mechanisms—none of the organizational behaviors that typically lead to success.

While a disruption can be achieved through cost value *or* experience value *or* platform value, a successful Occupy strategy normally re-quires combinatorial disruption. Only by combining all three forms of value can an organization prevail in the disruption battle for any length of time.

In the face of the disruption that online competitors like Casper and Endy are bringing to the mattress industry, an incumbent company, Sleep Country Canada, is thriving.[33] In 2018, Sleep Country reported double-digit sales growth and improving profitability, with strong rev-enue growth for 20 consecutive quarters.[34] CEO David Friesema ex-plained: "In a challenging retail environment, Sleep Country continues to perform well thanks to the efforts of our associates who every day create a great customer experience."

Far from retrenching, the company is aggressively investing, improving cost controls and inventory levels. It's expanding its 239-store presence across Canada by opening eight to 12 new stores per year starting in 2018. The company also plans to renovate 25 to 30 existing stores, increase advertising and marketing spend to improve its brand image, and continue to enhance the customer experience. Because the company has direct ownership of its stores, it can train employees to focus on service quality and maintaining an excellent customer experience. The company is also launching new product lines and expanding with simple products sold through an e-commerce channel. As a result, total revenue, market share (Sleep Country has an estimated 27 percent share of the Canadian mattress market), same-store sales, and profit margins are growing.[35]

Sleep Country Canada is also "disrupting the disruptors," emulating the market-changing innovations that underpin the value of Casper and Endy's offers, while continuing to wield its physical stores presence and greater bargaining strengths. It launched an easy-to-deliver mattress-in-a-box called Bloom,[36] allowing it to participate in a fast-growing segment of the market.[37] The company has always offered a 100-day satisfaction guarantee but is benefiting from the market awareness that online competitors' marketing efforts are creating.

It also launched a low-price foam mattress called "Bloom Earth,"[38] undercutting the low end of its online competitors' price range, while gradually building out its digital presence.[39] In addition, the company is starting a partnership with UK-based Simba,[40] a fast-growing start-up, to carry its premium "Hybrid" mattress-in-a-box brand.

By adopting the innovations that differentiated its online competitors, while simultaneously taking full advantage of the strengths associated with its physical retail footprint, Sleep Country Canada is consolidating its market position and continuing to grow—an example of a successful Occupy strategy.

Whereas Harvest and Retreat strategies are well-suited to more conventional change management approaches, offensive strategies like Disrupt and Occupy demand that organizations work in the Orchestration Zone, taking a highly connected approach to change, which we will detail in the coming pages.

At the DBT Center, we are often asked by executives, "What should we do first in our transformation program?" The answer is: start by establishing guiding objectives.

CHAPTER 3
Establishing Guiding Objectives of a Transformation

WHICH STRATEGY, WHEN?

With a solid understanding of guiding objectives, we can turn now to how these objectives should be instituted. How do you determine which strategy is appropriate? Or which forms of customer value should be prioritized? And how do guiding objectives set the stage for executing a transformation program?

Drawing on our research into digital transformation journeys, we have built a simple tool called "20 Questions" to help organizations prioritize strategic responses (see Figure 16).

Instructions: Below are four scorecards that correspond to the four strategies described in Chapter 2. Each has five questions, for a total of 20. Answer each question with a "Yes" or a "No." Then, add up the number of "Yes" responses for each strategy. Next, enter the total number of "Yes" answers from each scorecard at the bottom. The cell with the highest number of "Yes" responses is the dominant strategy. Remember, this should be done at the line-of-business level, not for your company overall.

Fig. 16: **20 Questions for Choosing the Right Strategy**

Harvest	Yes/No
Is this business coming under abnormal market pressure from disruptors?	
Does a value vampire, a disruptor whose competitive advantage shrinks overall revenues or profits, exist in this market?	
Can profits be retained or increased by using digitization to produce efficiencies and reduce costs that maintain competitiveness?	
Can disruptors be blocked (e.g., through a lawsuit, through aggressive marketing counter claims)?	
Do you believe this market will remain profitable for your company, even if revenues decline, for at least two years?	
Total number of "Yes" answers	

Retreat	Yes/No
Has this business passed an inflection point at which returns on capital are no longer attractive?	
Is it possible to maintain this business as a smaller but profitable niche serving specialized customers (that disruptors are not interested in) for at least two years?	
Are there synergies with other parts of the business that would make it attractive to keep this business going, even if it loses money (i.e., as a loss leader, to create some kind of customer "lock in")?	
Does this business have assets, intellectual property, processes, or talent that could be deployed elsewhere more profitably?	
Could you exit this business without incurring major costs, or could you sell the business?	
Total number of "Yes" answers	

Disrupt	Yes/No
Is there an opportunity to use digital technologies and business models to dramatically improve customer value in this business?	
Is there a way to reinvent value by bypassing a traditional value chain?	
Have you identified a new value vacancy – a market opportunity that can be profitably exploited via digital disruption?	
Are margins fat in this industry (à la Jeff Bezos's infamous remark that "your margin is my opportunity")?	
Can a new market be formed or an adjacent market entered in a way that allows you to leverage existing offerings or capabilities?	
Total number of "Yes" answers	

Occupy	Yes/No
Has a competitor already disrupted a market that is appealing to you?	
Is there a robust value vacancy that you can target?	
Is there a path to establish a durable position of market leadership?	
If you were the original disruptor (i.e., not someone else), do you need to change the offering or how you operate to reflect increased competition?	
Has there been a "next" disruption that disrupts the value vacancy in this market, meaning the whole landscape shifts?	
Total number of "Yes" answers	

Harvest	Retreat	Disrupt	Occupy

Source: Global Center for Digital Business Transformation, 2019

Few incumbents are "all in" on any one strategy because their business lines are usually numerous, diverse, and face variable levels of disruption. If your company is a large bank, for example, the level of disruption in commercial or wholesale banking might be utterly different from that found in consumer lending. Profit pools may be more or less secure, customer relationships more or less cemented, and value chains more or less ossified in different parts of the business. Therefore, a *portfolio approach* that balances defensive and offensive strategies is almost always warranted. Blending defensive and offensive strategies in this manner can also allay profitability crunches associated with transitioning too rapidly from one mature (but declining) business to another nascent (but fast-growing) business—that is, where the latter's high relative growth can't keep pace with the former's absolute dollar-volume decline.

However, certain strategies in the Strategic Response Playbook are employed more than others. Retreat strategies are less frequent, in part because, as we observed in our earlier book, leaders are reluctant to pursue them (out of fear they will be perceived as signposts of deficient leadership) and because, even though market entry and exit rates are accelerating in the

> A portfolio approach that balances defensive and offensive strategies is almost always warranted.

Digital Vortex, "wrapping up" a business is not a daily occurrence for firms. Similarly, Disrupt strategies are not something companies embark on frequently or lightly. They tend to be radical departures from what the company has done in the past and require a different model for market formation, incubation, and scaling.

Most incumbents are not good at Disrupt strategies because they imply being first to market, often with a small subset of early-adopter customers. For a lot of big companies, Disrupt strategies run the risk of becoming what Frederic Herren, senior vice president, digital and innovation at $6 billion Swiss testing, inspection, and verification service leader SGS SA, called "Sputnik initiatives." He was referring to foolhardy "moonshots" and "science experiments" the mainstream of the business is ambivalent about or, worse, is actively rooting against.

More commonly, big, traditional, prosperous companies concentrate their efforts on Harvest and Occupy. The former means playing defense, and usually involves a lot of cost optimization, streamlining, and specialization. The latter means playing offense, but after a value vacancy and a market disruption have already materialized, allowing the incumbent to be a "fast follower" and compete based on its unique strengths.

Figure 17 shows a typical distribution of strategies for a market incumbent. That doesn't mean that your strategy mix must look like this. It just means that most incumbents find that Harvest and Occupy are best suited to a majority of their business lines.

Fig. 17: Incumbents Need a Portfolio Approach to Strategy

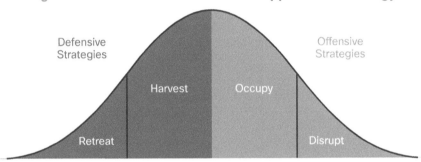

Source: Global Center for Digital Business Transformation, 2019

How do you know which kinds of customer value to create in a given business line? Should it be cost value, experience value, platform value, or all three, a combinatorial disruption?

Actually, you have already taken a step toward the answer: you have chosen a strategy of Harvest, Retreat, Disrupt, or Occupy. In doing so, you determine which forms of value to pursue. Customer value creation cannot be dissociated from these strategies—it's their very substance. Figure 18 illustrates how customer value creation and strategic response work together.

Fig. 18: How Customer Value Creation Relates to Strategy

		DEFENSIVE STRATEGIES		OFFENSIVE STRATEGIES	
		Harvest	Retreat	Disrupt	Occupy
$	Cost Value	✓	✓	✓ (hollow)	✓
				or...	and...
⏱	Experience Value	✓	✓	✓	✓
				or...	and...
👥	Platform Value			✓	✓

Source: Global Center for Digital Business Transformation, 2016-2019

If you are playing defense, you will normally want to concentrate value creation in cost value or experience value, making the market tougher for disruptive competitors by leveraging the strengths of your incumbency. On offense, Disrupt strategies for incumbents rarely involve creating a lot of cost value (you don't want to disrupt the economics of a profitable business for no reason; hence, the hollow check mark in Figure 18). But if the market disruption is completely new, and no legacy business will be cannibalized, cost value can play a role for incumbents in Disrupt. Experience value and platform value are the most common value-creation focuses for big companies pursuing a Disrupt strategy. However, any one of the three forms of value can be the basis of Disrupt.

In Occupy, incumbents need to deliver all three forms of value to keep customers from migrating to competitors who are similarly targeting the value vacancy—and to secure the continued status of market leader.

Formulating guiding objectives is not tidy or linear. To compete effectively, incumbents need to be customer value-obsessed, just as disruptive competitors are. Disruptors use new business models to optimize how they create, deliver, and capture that value. Big traditional companies must follow suit.

But disruptors have a much simpler task when it comes to guiding objectives. They have no risk of undercutting existing businesses, and managing maturing businesses alongside high-growth products and services is not a concern. Often, they don't even have profits to protect. For incumbents, the guiding objectives challenge is far more acute, and making changes is orders of magnitude more complex.

FROM GUIDING OBJECTIVES TO EXECUTION: INTUIT

The three components of guiding objectives—customer value creation, business models, and strategy—cannot be developed sequentially. To frame execution, they must be considered as an integrated whole.

A case in point is Intuit, the Mountain View, California-based business and financial software and services firm. With 2017 revenues topping $6 billion, Intuit is best known for its consumer and small-business offerings such as QuickBooks and TurboTax.[1] Founded in 1983, the firm has retained a consistent vision: to provide consumers and small businesses with offers that simplify the complex financial decisions of their lives.[2]

Albert "Al" Ko, Intuit's chief transformation officer, told us that "transformation has to be in service of a strategy, and I don't believe that strategy is a cost-savings target per se."

Through comprehensive "strategy refresh" exercises, the company has successfully anticipated major disruptions in its market over the past few decades. Every three to four years, Intuit conducts reviews of market shifts and changing customer demands. It also examines the alignment of its activities and structure and responds to the strategic implications of major trends that might affect its competitiveness.

Using this approach, the company establishes clear strategic directions for pursuing growth and driving organizational change—and it revisits them regularly. The strategy refresh is not done entirely in response to specific disruptions but is viewed as a normal part of business. Intuit transforms on an ongoing basis, even during high-growth periods—what Intuit's CEO calls "fixing the roof while the sun is shining."

Customer value creation is the basis of the strategy refresh. "If we figure out how to simplify customers' financial lives, then we can create a great business by delivering customer benefits," said Ko. "And I'll come back to that term 'customer benefits.' It's a very critical thing for us and part of our lexicon from the early days. 'Are we delivering on what the largest customer problems are?'" Intuit has become renowned for its ability to develop new forms of experience value by delivering solutions to the financial complexity faced by individuals and small-business owners.

Customer value creation depends on an in-depth understanding of value chains, business models, and the competitive landscape. In recent years, Intuit saw encroachment from disruptors like Zoho Books and big tech companies such as Microsoft. In response, Intuit decided to confront the Digital Vortex head on. As Ko put it, "External market insights led to strategic implications for Intuit, which led to a wholesale, and sometimes painful, reorganization of our entire company, from the leaders to the functional groups to resource allocation."

In 2012, for example, the company decided to expand through a cloud-based software delivery model and by penetrating international markets. Its analysis had highlighted social, mobile, cloud, and data as crucial. Intuit decided to deliver everything its customers did via a mobile device—at a time when most of its revenue came from desktop software like TurboTax, which was purchased in shrink-wrapped packages at retailers such as Fry's Electronics, Staples, and Costco. The company invested in cloud-driven services, data security and privacy, providing a consistent worldwide user experience, all ahead of the industry's software-as-a-service (SaaS) shift.

Intuit was now positioned to deliver a true combinatorial disruption to customers, blending cost value, experience value, and platform value. Affordably priced SaaS offers for QuickBooks Online (QBO) and TurboTax created cost value for customers interested in a subscription payment. Experience value came from the ability to use the applications on mobile devices, to integrate accounting and tax processes seamlessly, to handle collaboration between a small business and third parties such as accountants, to personalize the application for international users, and to receive frictionless upgrades.

Integrating QBO with other ecosystem offers such as financing and loans management, tax processing, and sales account collaboration effectively made it an open platform for the suppliers on which small and midsized businesses rely, creating platform value. For example, QBO 2011 and 2012 offered integration with Salesforce.com's customer relationship management solutions.[3]

With this combinatorial disruption, Intuit gave small companies the ability to benefit from the same type of finance and accounting integration once reserved for large companies that could spend millions on enterprise resource planning systems. This combination of value virtually tripled Intuit's total addressable market from less than $20 billion to north of $55 billion in 2017.[4]

In doing so, Intuit adopted an Occupy strategy: the launch of an advantageously priced TurboTax cloud offer quickly displaced the desktop version of its tax software.[5] Intuit was willing to cannibalize its own product to build a large market share with a cloud-based product that ensured much more loyalty from customers. This prevented a competitor, Microsoft, from capturing a significant portion of the market with its Microsoft Money software. In fact, Microsoft interrupted that offer and stopped supporting it altogether after 2011.[6]

Time after time, Intuit's external market insights drove its prioritization efforts. From eight lines of business in 2010, including units delivering services to the financial and healthcare industries, Intuit chose to prioritize just two major markets: the consumer and small-business segments. It reallocated most of its resources to these customers and divested from the other segments—a Retreat strategy.

This portfolio approach to strategy reflected the opportunities and threats facing each business line. Whereas 90 percent of the company's revenue once came from on-premise, desktop software, the company grew its QuickBooks mobile SaaS customer base from 360,000 to 3.5 million in a six-year span. All the while, it expanded rapidly outside the United States and Canada into seven other countries.

In late 2017, the company began its next strategy refresh cycle. Seeing data analytics, AI, and machine learning as the new disruptive capabilities likely to impact customer experiences, Intuit mobilized over 100 teams to review research on trends and customer feedback. Based on this, Ko and the management team identified eight major macro trends driving massive societal and economic shifts. In response, the company is reallocating $1 billion—roughly one-fourth of its operating expenses—to address these opportunities.

Under the leadership of Al Ko, Intuit's recurring strategy refresh is becoming a repeatable process. Using knowledge and best practices from the past two iterations in 2012 and 2017, his team is codifying them in the company's operating rhythm. The process of revisiting the strategy and assessing its progress is now fully represented in the company's one- and three-year planning cycles, and in operating reviews. But Ko insists that regardless of how repeatable the refresh has become, there's no substitute for revisiting a massive list of trends and opportunities regularly and stress-testing ways to create more value for customers.

Intuit provides a compelling example of how transformation is an essential and *perpetual* task of leadership. Investors seem to like the results of Ko's "maniacal focus" on strategy refresh, and the execution that has followed. Intuit's market capitalization has increased by roughly 600 percent since 2010, compared with some 250 percent for the Nasdaq overall.[7]

> A transformation ambition is a statement that outlines the company's overall change goal. It aggregates the strategic intent of all the guiding objectives that span the company's divisions or businesses, unifying the aims of the transformation to promote aligned execution.

TRANSFORMATION AMBITION

If guiding objectives must be set at the line-of-business level, what does this mean in terms of "company-wide" transformation? Recalling Figure 10, where we introduced the idea of the Orchestration Zone, isn't digital business transformation something that is inherently pan-enterprise?

This leads us to another important concept that is related to, but distinct from, guiding objectives: the company's **transformation ambition.** This is simply a statement that outlines the company's *overall change goal*. The transformation ambition aggregates the strategic intent of *all the guiding objectives that span the company's divisions or businesses,* unifying the aims of the transformation to promote aligned execution. This is not a vague mission statement (internal) or brand promise (external) but is instead focused on what the competitive state of the company will be at some defined point in the future, usually a few years out.

Good transformation ambitions have a few consistent characteristics, which we describe with the acronym "PRISM," as shown in Figure 19. They act as a "prism" that focuses and directs the organization's energies.

Fig. 19: Characteristics of a Good Transformation Ambition

Transformation Ambition

Precise
Realistic
Inclusive
Succinct
Measurable

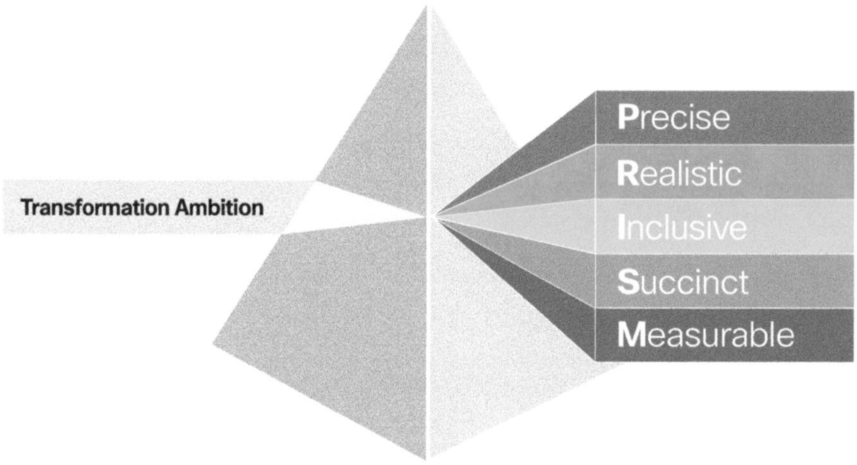

Source: Global Center for Digital Business Transformation, 2019

The transformation ambition must be *precise*. It has to be unambiguous, with no room for interpretation. This helps everyone understand the target state.

The transformation ambition has to be *realistic*. It has to be something executive leadership, middle management, and individual contributors all can credibly see the company actually pulling off. It can't be pie in the sky.

It also has to be *inclusive*. It needs to be relevant to everyone in the company, from top to bottom, and from side to side. It has to be comprehensive, bracketing the guiding objectives of all the company's businesses.

It has to be *succinct*. It must be something the average employee can easily remember, almost a rallying cry. It can't be so complex that it covers everything conceivably relevant. It's a description of a destination, not a laundry list of all the steps required to get there. A succinct, easy-to-recall transformation ambition enables everyone during the course of their work to gauge whether what they are doing, in fact, supports the established end goal.

Finally, the transformation ambition must be *measurable*. It can't be so squishy that everyone can define progress in his or her own way. There have to be consistent metrics that allow the organization to pinpoint where it is on its journey, and what remains to be accomplished. It also must be time-bound.

Transformation ambitions that embody the PRISM characteristics help steer decision-making and execution. Unfortunately, many corporate articulations of purpose amount to little more than window-dressing—what the late US President George H.W. Bush famously referred to dismissively as "the vision thing."[8] These messages may work as inspirational posters in the company cafeteria but have little relevance for people who make decisions or are asked to execute a complex change in the business. Visions like "we aspire to be the most admired company in our industry" fit this mold. It's not that they're wrong or inappropriate, it's just that they do not act as lenses that can focus execution.

Cisco provides a good example of a strong transformation ambition. The company's *mission statement* reflects the company's overall values and vision: "Shape the future of the internet by creating unprecedented value and opportunity for our customers, employees, investors, and ecosystem partners."[9]

However, the company's *transformation ambition* was something else: 40/40/2020. This was a shorthand leaders used to describe a future standing in which the company would garner 40 percent of its revenue from recurring (subscription-based) sources and 40 percent from software by the year 2020 (the company's 2021 fiscal year). The transformation ambition met all these criteria—it was precise, realistic, inclusive, succinct, and measurable.

The transformation ambition of 40/40/2020 was not a commitment to Wall Street, but rather a kind of unofficial, universally understood "north star" for the company. Although these numbers evolved slightly over time to reflect the state of the business (in fact, they were revised upward), the transformation ambition galvanized activities on multiple fronts. While transformation of Cisco's enterprise networking business looked different from its security or collaboration businesses, across the board, transformation efforts were prioritized, formulated, and executed in service of this broader transformation ambition that had been set by the company's CEO, CFO, and executive leadership.

When Dr. Mathias Döpfner was made CEO of Axel Springer SE in 2002, the situation he faced was dire. Axel Springer was the largest print media company in Germany, owning or controlling many of the nation's largest newspapers and magazines. Media properties like *Bild* and *Die Welt* were, and still are, part of its portfolio. When Döpfner took over, Axel Springer earned revenues from four major sources: sales, subscriptions, advertising, and classifieds, all of which were in decline.

In 2004, he articulated a bold transformation ambition for the firm. He declared that 50 percent of revenues and profits would come from digital sources within a decade. As with Cisco, this transformation ambition acted as a compass for the entire group and framed how all organizational changes would be executed. (A transformation ambition doesn't have to be so "numerical," as those of Cisco and Axel Springer were, but should reflect the PRISM characteristics.)

By any reasonable measure, this was an audacious goal for Axel Springer. At the time, digital media accounted for about 3 percent of revenues—and there were no digital profits. Many observers, inside and outside the company, didn't think the goal was achievable. Yet

Axel Springer reached both the top-line and bottom-line goals two years ahead of schedule.[10] When the 10-year mark arrived in 2014, more than 50 percent of group revenues and 70 percent of profits were coming from digital sources.[11]

GETTING WITH THE PROGRAM

Throughout its journey, Axel Springer referred back to a precise, realistic, inclusive, succinct, and measurable transformation ambition that steered its execution. Transformation ambitions like these can be enormously helpful in one vital area: keeping everyone on side.

Creating and sustaining leadership consensus around the direction of a digital business transformation was an issue our interviewees returned to again and again. As Michelle Ash, chief innovation officer at the $8 billion Canadian mining leader Barrick Gold, explained, once companies move past the more basic, efficiency-oriented digitization activities (i.e., the types that fall into the Change Management Zone), transformation practitioners begin to encounter resistance:

> You then start touching so many areas of the business that you've got to get people right from the board and executives, general management, supervisors, all the way down to the operators involved, engaged, and understanding. That has with it quite a few challenges in terms of how you convince different groups of people that the change that you're about to make is the right one, is good for them, and they can deal with it. There are all sorts of organizational antibodies at different levels that want to keep the organization the way it was in some way, shape, or form.

This is typical. Very often, influential forces are arrayed against a digital business transformation. This can manifest as opposition to the overall strategic direction the transformation represents, or as a lack of agreement on what should be done about it—that is, how the transformation should be brought about and the division of labor. As Karl Walsh, CDO and senior vice president of e-commerce for the $4 billion Danish jewelry manufacturer and retailer PANDORA A/S, noted in our conversation, "Absolute clarity up front of who does what and what we mean by this digital transformation is critical."

If a firm cannot achieve consensus among its executive leadership, transformation is likely to go sideways before it goes ahead. It may even stall completely. A powerful faction among the executive team, which must include the CEO and the board, is needed to overcome resistance to change. A CEO and board, backed by cooperative leaders, must establish an unambiguous stance supporting the transformation ambition.

Waddaah Keirbeck, CIO at $2.2 billion American commercial payment solution provider FLEETCOR, echoed this view: "My philosophy was, we were clear on what we're trying to do and why. It was not a choice, it was, 'Leadership defined this vision, this is what we're going to do. We know it's not going to be easy, but either help, or get out of the way.'"

As a whole, the organization will scrutinize leadership for any indication from the upper echelons that the transformation is a passing fancy or "just another fire drill," or that it's OK for managers and front-line employees to opt out. It's essential, therefore, for those upper echelons to consistently reinforce the transformation ambition in their communications, and to ensure the business line-level guiding objectives are transparent.

For example, to initiate change at the $68 billion German automaker Audi AG, "we started with senior management—motivating and inspiring them to advocate for change," said former Audi AG CIO Mattias Ulbrich. "We consistently reminded teams within IT and the business units of our overarching transformation goals. And through our use of competence networks, we have facilitated a permanent dialogue between business and IT teams. In this way, change can cascade from key transformation agents to the entire organization."[12]

Metrics also play an important role in the ongoing management of a transformation program, quantifying and tracking progress (or the lack thereof) against guiding objectives and the transformation ambition. One CDO told us, "We invest heavily in measurement to drive accountability. Data means there is nowhere to hide. If you're not on side, there won't be a sliver of daylight."

This can be crucial for ensuring consistent alignment and execution. As Patrick Hoffstetter, former CDO of $68 billion French automotive giant Renault, put it: "We have to come up with figures, KPIs, benchmarks, and so on to show we are not pushing [the transformation] to look modern or because it's trendy but because it's really impacting the business."[13]

GETTING ROLLING

At this stage, we'd like to introduce you to an imaginary company, BikeCo, a leading manufacturer and retailer of bicycles (see sidebar). We'll be along for the ride, so to speak, during BikeCo's transformation journey, which will be charted over the next several chapters.

BikeCo has been a successful incumbent for the past 40 years, and one of the top three US bicycle firms in terms of market share for most of the past two decades. It's neither a top-of-the-line nor a "cheap-and-cheerful" low-end competitor. It sits in the middle of the market, selling traditional road bikes, bicycle components, repair services, and accessories.

The company's market has seen considerable change in recent years. Disruptive business models such as bike sharing have begun to see traction. New market entrants from China, South Korea, and India offer competitive, aggressively priced products. Custom-

Meet BikeCo

BikeCo was founded in the mid-1970s by an amateur road-racing enthusiast who had worked as an engineer for a major aerospace company. The founder began selling road bike frames out of his garage and opened his first bike shop after just one year in business. The popularity of his designs grew rapidly among professional and amateur racers, who found that the bikes' innovative, lightweight designs set them apart from the heavy steel-frame products that were on the market.

Over the next three decades, the company opened several dozen retail stores, all acting as BikeCo-certified service centers, and grew to more than 2,000 employees. BikeCo is headquartered in Massachusetts and maintains one factory in the Netherlands (from its largest acquisition) and two in Taiwan. Most of its sales come from distribution partners, including more than 1,200 independent bike shops and a number of retail

(Continued on next page)

Meet BikeCo

(Continued from previous page)

chains. It operates mainly in the United States with a minor presence in Europe.

Key lines of business include:
- Fully-assembled road bikes
- Bicycle components
- Aftermarket services
- Accessories

In its most recent fiscal year, the company reported annual sales of $1.1 billion, representing a 10 percent share of the overall US market, down from 14 percent during the preceding year. Margins decreased by 6.8 percent during the year, a decline the company attributed to aggressive pricing from large European bike brand conglomerates and new Asian competitors with low-cost models.

er demands for new hybrid models, which combine road and mountain bike features, and for electric-assist bikes have prompted a lot of scrambling to innovate and create new offerings. In addition, big mergers among brands in Europe and Asia have roiled the marketplace, while emerging competitors targeting the American market have leveraged world-class digital capabilities in development, supply chain, and distribution to improve designs and drive down costs. As a result, last year, BikeCo saw its business take a major dip for the first time, dropping from third to sixth place in terms of US market share. Profits also declined sharply.

Alarm bells were ringing in the company's executive offices. Management commissioned a detailed analysis of the market and BikeCo's competitive position. The analysis revealed long-term softness in its core road bike business. In the United States, growth was concentrated in the mountain bike and new hybrid markets, where the company had next to no brand equity or momentum. Its only mountain bike product, introduced eight years ago, fizzled.

The analysis suggested, however, that BikeCo's channel sales model presented some important advantages. Although it had more than 40 branded BikeCo retail stores in major US metropolitan areas, its business was overwhelmingly conducted through retail partners, mostly small bicycle retailing chains and individual shops loyal to the BikeCo brand. BikeCo was also an early adopter of e-commerce capabilities. It had built a multimillion dollar business in online retailing of BikeCo helmets, jerseys, locks, and other merchandise. Perhaps most important, it had a large and mostly captive audience of bike shops that resold BikeCo component parts such as brakes, shifters, and cranksets. BikeCo's component business and its distribution model were a major competitive differentiator.

The company decided it needed a bold move to match the pressure placed on the market by Asian competitors. Historically, most of the customer value that the firm offered was experience value. With the average price of a BikeCo road bike hovering around $900, the company was not focused on helping customers create an economic gain of some kind, or enjoy a dramatically lower price. Instead, it aimed to create a great ownership experience, with a trusted name, high-quality products, and a brand associated with road racing through sponsorships, events, and other promotions.

To augment this, the company began thinking about new ways to create value for customers. The idea of a platform model was floated, and a working group was formed to hatch a business plan to create a BikeCo-led platform play.

The plan called for BikeCo to offer an exchange-based business model to customers, suppliers, and retail partners. The company would create a new digital revenue stream by charging suppliers and retail partners a 10 percent transaction fee for each sale of replacement parts that occurred on the platform. This was a major departure for BikeCo. It represented a new-to-the-market disruption; no one else had a platform like this. The company planned to connect customers and partners, so they could share information and conduct commerce in replacement bike parts, with BikeCo brokering the exchanges. BikeCo branded the digital platform "BikeCo SHIFT."

Thus, BikeCo's guiding objectives for its components business looked like this:

Customer value creation: Platform value, leading to combinatorial disruption. By connecting customers, suppliers, and retailers in a digital marketplace business model, BikeCo SHIFT created value for everyone involved. The power of this platform *also* allowed the company to enhance other forms of customer value. It created a combinatorial disruption that could shake up the industry and reposition BikeCo at the center. The BikeCo SHIFT platform lowered overall costs for end customers (cost value) and created more choice and new channels for sourcing components for buyers and sellers (experience value).

Strategy: Disrupt. Despite its status as a market incumbent, BikeCo was able to harness digital technologies and combine them with a digital marketplace business model to create a completely new approach for bike component sales, leveraging the company's ecosystem. This is a Disrupt strategy.

The BikeCo SHIFT platform provoked a lot of discussion among the management team. Were they taking full advantage of digital? BikeCo SHIFT was looking like a game-changer for their components business. But what about the core business of selling assembled road bikes? Leaders from the company's other lines of business reframed their own guiding objectives. Based on the competition they were seeing, they resolved to win back market share by digitizing key processes in the core business. This would allow BikeCo to lower costs and fight off "good enough" alternatives from overseas competitors. A major focus would be making the lives of their retail distributors easier with new digital ordering and fulfillment processes.

> Appendix 1 is our "Digital Disruption Diagnostic," which can help you establish guiding objectives at your company. It provides an intuitive tool for charting a business's approach to customer value creation, relevant business models, and the right strategy, today and in the future.

Customer value for these business lines would focus mainly on cost value for end customers and the experience value that would come from operational simplification for its retail channel. These lines of business were not pursuing platform value or an offensive Disrupt strategy. They were using a defensive strategy: Harvest. BikeCo, therefore, was employing a portfolio of strategies that was optimized for the opportunities and threats facing their different lines of business.

The management team realized that, with all this change going on, they needed a way to cement and communicate their overall competitive direction. Their transformation ambition became "50 in 4 by 25," a shorthand that meant BikeCo aimed to earn 50 percent of its revenues from digital channels across all four lines of business by 2025. This transformation ambition was precise, realistic, inclusive, succinct, and measurable. It created clarity for everyone in the company on what success looked like and how they should prioritize their work.

The advent of the BikeCo SHIFT platform required a true digital business transformation. As we'll demonstrate in the pages ahead, BikeCo's platform business would require massive changes in how the company operates and in its organizational resources. Making this happen was a huge challenge that would require BikeCo to undertake change in the Orchestration Zone.

Now let's assume your company, like BikeCo, has set guiding objectives for its businesses. It has identified the new, compelling value proposition it will offer to customers (or how it intends to optimize the value it already provides), and the business models needed to make this value a reality. It has also defined the portfolio of strategies, both defensive and offensive, that it plans to carry out in the different markets it serves. It has connected its guiding objectives to articulate to all its stakeholders a transformation ambition that can act as a touchstone for all the work that follows. Finally, it has pushed a sturdy leadership consensus on this strategic direction into the business.

We have seen that many change efforts break down because of poorly defined guiding objectives and a lack of understanding about the organization's target competitive state. With guiding objectives and the company's overall transformation ambition now in place, the organization is ready to orchestrate a connected approach to change.

CHAPTER 4
The Transformation Orchestra

INSTRUMENTS OF CHANGE

In 2015 and 2016, we chose the image of a vortex to conceptualize and explain the market change we were witnessing and hearing about from executives. In the physical world, a vortex has certain qualities that help us understand what's happening in the digital world. These qualities—exponentially increasing speed; chaos and uncertainty; and inexorable convergence—were brought to life by the vortex metaphor, helping us think about *market* change. In the same vein, the metaphor of a symphony orchestra can help us conceptualize and explain *organizational* change.

If you imagine an organization as an orchestra, you can see how orchestration works. Think of a company as being composed of instruments, grouped in sections. Together, they perform a piece of music. The different instruments all contribute to a harmonious and successful performance.

It may be helpful here to recall our definition of "orchestrate"—*to mobilize and enable so as to achieve a desired effect.* This is exactly what a conductor does when leading an orchestra. The maestro directs the activities of the musicians to produce a performance that reflects the very best of their abilities. Collectively, their performances should make the whole greater than the sum of the parts.

For a firm, establishing guiding objectives is like composing a musical piece—one that calls on each section (e.g., strings, brass, woodwinds) of the orchestra to play its part at the appropriate time. Once the company has composed its musical piece—i.e., after it has charted its desired competitive state for the future—it must bring the composition to life. In other words, it must execute.

But how do you "play" the music? Even the most beautiful score will sound like a cacophony if the instruments all play at once or if the musicians are not "all on the same page."

The guiding objectives, which represent direction at the line-of-business level, are the "movements" of the symphony. Collectively, they form the transformation ambition, which is the entire symphony that your company wants to perform.

We've dubbed this framework the **Transformation Orchestra,** an analogy in which eight instruments of a musical orchestra correspond to eight organizational elements in a company (see Figure 20).[i] Each element contains important considerations for leaders, such as the company's go-to-market model, how it engages stakeholders, and how it's organized. The Transformation Orchestra is a construct that helps leaders think in a "post-functional" way, moving past organizational silos to activate all the resources that must come together to achieve the company's aims.

Instruments are logical groupings of organizational resources that align to a particular business imperative, such as launching a new offering, delivering a new digital customer experience, or changing the company's culture. An instrument represents all the organizational resources from across the business that must be orchestrated to address a transformation challenge.

Instruments are logical groupings of organizational resources that align to a particular business imperative, such as launching a new

---

i   Note that the "sheet music" shown in this framework does not depict the company's transformation ambition—only its guiding objectives. This is because orchestration should be "conducted" at the line-of-business level. The transformation ambition is something larger. It spans all the company's businesses and serves as a reference for aligning execution in a holistic sense. Guiding objectives, by contrast, focus on connecting the organization to address a specific opportunity or threat. They also highlight the challenges that come with adapting the business to these opportunities and threats. And, for the sake of brevity, the sheet music doesn't show which business models are used to create, capture, and deliver value. As explained earlier, business models are what operationalize cost value, experience value, and platform value. Therefore, business models are implicit in this framework.

offering, delivering a new digital customer experience, or changing the company's culture. An instrument represents all the organizational resources from across the business that must be orchestrated to address a transformation challenge. Note that instruments are *not* the same as departments or functions, a point on which we will elaborate in the pages ahead.

Fig. 20: **The Transformation Orchestra**

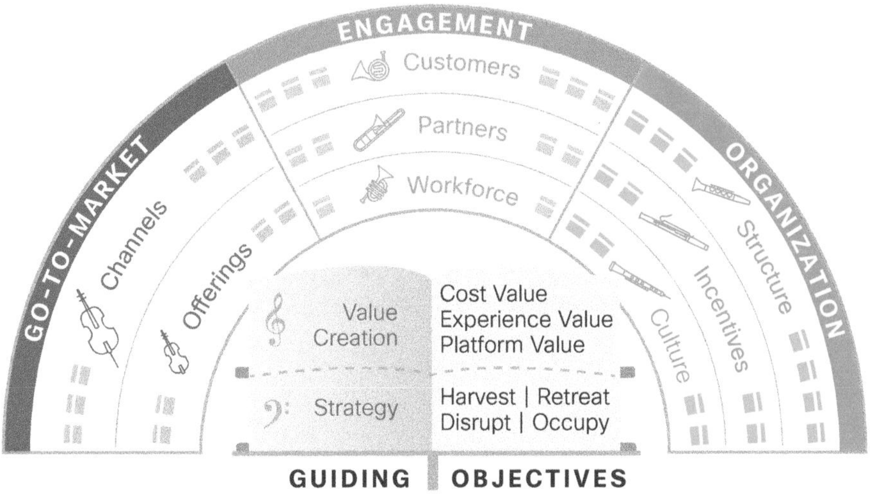

Source: Global Center for Digital Business Transformation, 2019

Like a bravura orchestral performance, a successful digital business transformation engages the eight instruments when and where they are needed. Although companies must prioritize and sequence the areas that need to be transformed, good orchestration involves more than this (for example, you rarely hear just the stringed instruments, followed by just the horns, playing in sequence).

As with a musical piece, a digital business transformation usually requires different organizational elements to work *in concert*–simultaneously and collaboratively. While a violin solo can be powerful, a single instrument produces far less impact than a full orchestra. Organizations that change only their offerings (for example, by adding connectivity to a product) tend to achieve limited impacts. According to our research, the best transformations–those with the highest odds for success—are holistic. They encompass the *entire* organization and *all* its resources.

The instruments we've identified as the core of the Transformation Orchestra are the product of hundreds of interactions with executives since the inception of the DBT Center. Through these engagements, we've determined that the success or failure of a transformation hinges on balancing the requirements of these eight instruments, spanning three sections of the Transformation Orchestra.

Go-to-Market Section

1. **Offerings:** The products and services your company sells.

2. **Channels:** How products and services reach customers (i.e., route to market).

Engagement Section

3. **Customer Engagement:** How your company engages with its customers.

4. **Partner Engagement:** How your company engages with its partner ecosystem.

5. **Workforce Engagement:** How your company engages with its employees and contract staff.

Organization Section

6. **Org Structure:** The structure of business units, teams, reporting lines, and profit and loss centers (P&Ls).

7. **Incentives:** How workers are compensated and rewarded for their performance and behavior.

8. **Culture:** The values, attitudes, beliefs, and habits of the company.

Part of the power of the Transformation Orchestra is in setting the boundaries of a transformation. For many executives, digital business transformation is murky, abstract, and unnerving. They aren't sure what's in and out of scope, or where to start. Demonstrating that the focus should be on *eight* elements (not three, not 40) is liberating. It provides scope and structure to the task of executing organizational change in the service of guiding objectives.

SOLOS AND SILOS

Transformation programs founder when organizations fail to appreciate the inherent connectedness of change. Figure 21 shows that most business leaders cite organizational silos as a major obstacle in executing a transformation.

Fig. 21: Silos Inhibit Execution

Survey Q. To what degree do organizational silos inhibit your organization's ability to execute a transformation?

17% Significant degree

42% Considerable degree

29% Moderate degree

9% Slight degree

3% Not at all

N=1,030

Source: Global Center for Digital Business Transformation, 2019

Why does transforming just one part of the business not work? Doesn't it make sense to get "quick wins"? Shouldn't we strive to "put points on the board"? Shouldn't we incubate small-scale pilots first, and "focus on what we can control"? Isn't there a risk of being overwhelmed by the sheer magnitude of the challenge?

Transforming one part of the business *does* work if your aim is Plain Old Change or Smart X, two types of organizational change that are restricted to narrow functional areas (the two quadrants in the bottom half of Figure 10).

But when you're operating in the Orchestration Zone, pursuing digital business transformation at scale, you need a different approach. To illustrate, let's consider two of the instruments we've identified—Incentives and Org Structure—to show why the connectedness that goes with successful orchestration matters so much.

Would it make sense for your company to transform incentives and nothing else? When asked this way, it almost seems strange, and probably no sane manager would do this. Yet, the executives we've met often say that incentives are the key to changing behaviors and advancing execution. This isn't surprising, given that the business leaders we meet are capitalists who believe in the profit motive and capital accumulation. "Show them how it affects their pay" is an oft-heard mantra when discussing how to effect change.

Incentives have their place, but they should not be dealt with in a vacuum. Like all the instruments in the Transformation Orchestra, incentives are valuable only in how they influence other aspects of the firm and its execution.

As one transformation practitioner put it, "Imagine I put you in a room with a grand piano and a million dollars. I told you that you could have that million dollars if you could just play the piano for me. If you never had piano lessons in your life, you wouldn't be able to do it, no matter how hard you tried. At best, you might be able to bang out 'Chopsticks.' So, incentives are key, but should not be confused with real enablement."

Similarly, does it make sense to transform a company's organizational structure by itself? To see why this solution would be unhelpful vis-à-vis a transformation program, let's compare a large incumbent company with a major city—like London.

London is a bustling metropolis, rich in history and diversity. It's a place of great economic activity...and a real mess. Anyone who's ever driven a car in the city will attest that getting anywhere in London traffic can be a nightmare. A root-cause analysis of London's traffic woes is beyond our scope, but even a casual observer can see that much of the congestion stems from how the city's roads are structured.

London largely looks the way it does because of its past. Today's roads follow cart paths that date back to the Middle Ages, and even earlier to the Roman settlement of Londinium in the 1st century AD. They were certainly not designed to accommodate motor vehicles and the rapid population growth London has witnessed since the Industrial Revolution.

If we think of a big market incumbent as London, we can see the challenge of changing organizational structure by itself. How difficult and costly would it be to change the structure of London's roads into, say, an efficient system of streets modeled on low-congestion urban plans like those of Baltimore, Brasilia, or Budapest—cities where congestion levels are roughly half those of London?[1]

There are countless, well, "roadblocks."

Imagine knocking down buildings left, right, and center throughout London's financial and tourist centers, and building an organized grid of streets in the name of a "better" structure. The costs would be prohibitive, and you can bet local residents and business owners would not greet this plan warmly.

Today's incumbents are characterized by labyrinthine structures. They resemble those of London—like a rabbit warren that no one would ever design knowing what we know today. (By contrast, think about disruptors that are "greenfield" operations or "digital natives," and how vastly different they look to most big companies.) Fixing a company's structure for a modern environment like the Digital Vortex is no small task. It should not be done without reference to other areas of the business. Simply bulldozing walls in the name of digital is too expensive and too time-consuming.

The idea that reorgs are the key to transformation is a seductive misapprehension. One CDO we met with said, "Reorgs are what we do when we don't know what to do. But it feels good to be doing *something.*"

Emphasizing structural change in transformation programs, especially early on, is a mistake we've observed again and again across industries—one that often leads to a frustratingly low return on transformation investments. Instead, our recommendation is to make changes to organizational structure in a way that considers the impacts on other "instruments" in the company and the overall guiding objectives—not as a function of personalities or fiefdoms, or in pursuit of a dubious "reset" that will fix everything.

One practitioner described a phenomenon he called "previous idiot syndrome"—*everything that was done by the old regime must be*

Zappos: A Sole Focus in Transformation

Long known as a trailblazer, footwear retailer Zappos, a subsidiary of Amazon, has made various lists of "best companies to work for." In 2013, CEO Tony Hsieh began rolling out a new management approach called "Holacracy." In this model, the organization eliminated all hierarchy and bosses. Work progressed through a codified process that involved specialized meetings and ways of collaborating. All strategic decisions were tracked through a centralized application called GlassFrog.

Although Holacracy received extensive media attention in publications such as *The Wall Street Journal* and the *Harvard Business Review,* the results of the initiative were disastrous. Scrapping bosses, titles, and other traditional company structures created a lot of confusion and uncertainty for workers. What's more, the management approach was so rigid and artificial that many employees complained of being treated like cogs in a machine. Trust and camaraderie plummeted.

(Continued on next page)

wrong because I'm here and they're not. Don't change the org structure just to make it different from that of your predecessor. That's not transformation.

Changes to organizational structure should be made in a contextualized and connected manner. The best way to accomplish this is to address the issue through an orchestration-oriented approach. This applies not only to org structure but to everything you'd ever need to transform a company at scale. Focusing on one instrument in isolation is one of the most common errors we've observed in how transformation programs are executed (see sidebar).

ORGANIZATIONAL RESOURCES

An instrument is not a function like procurement or finance or marketing. For example, Workforce Engagement, one of the eight instruments in the orchestra, is not purely an HR issue, although many of the resources involved may "come from" that function. Similarly, Customer Engagement doesn't just involve the sales organization. Because most of us have been steeped in hierarchical and linear bureaucratic structures (think of a classical org chart), our minds are conditioned to form and fence in groups that reflect these structures.

Instruments are collections of organizational resources aligned to business outcomes, which must be brought to bear to execute change. They comprise three types of resources: people, data, and infrastructure (see Figure 22).

People are the individuals and teams needed to execute change. To effect a change in the company's offerings, for example, you might draw on people from R&D, product marketing, manufacturing, finance, a services organization (to support the offering), distribution and more. All these people are, or can be, oriented toward a business imperative associated with changing offerings. The needed people don't reside in a particular silo; they span the whole organization.

Data is the information needed to make a change. If a firm like BikeCo wants to move into the platform world and build an online exchange connecting end customers and partners, there is a lot of information that must be harnessed from across the company, as well as from the ecosystem that will use the platform. This information could include customer data, partner data, pricing data, product performance data, com-

petitive offer data, real-time data about relevant systems (e.g., transaction engines, web servers), data on supply chain events, and much, much more. Again, the needed data doesn't reside in a particular silo but spans the whole organization.

Infrastructure is all the "stuff" needed to make the change. Infrastructure represents tangible things—things you can stub your toe on—that can be used to execute change. They include facilities (e.g., offices, warehouses, contact centers), capital equipment (e.g., plant-floor equipment, vehicle fleets, machines), and especially IT assets

Zappos: A Sole Focus in Transformation

(Continued from previous page)

By 2015, employee turnover topped 30 percent, imperiling the company's competitive standing.[2]

Today, this experiment in driving transformation via org structure is widely regarded as a flop. However, we don't believe that the lesson lies in the management approach itself, but rather in the strategy of isolating transformation to one area of the business—to one instrument in the orchestra. Without an orchestration-centric approach that synchronized instruments such as Culture, Incentives, and Workforce Engagement, Zappos was tilting at windmills.

(e.g., computers, mobile devices, data center hardware). Once again, the needed things don't reside in a particular silo but span the whole organization.

Fig. 22: Instruments Consist of Organizational Resources

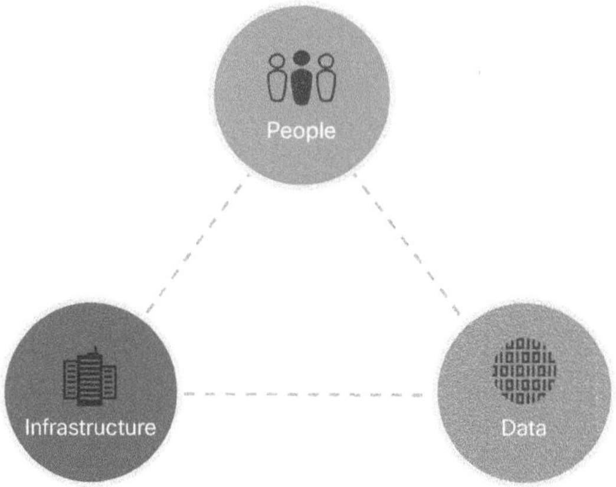

Source: Global Center for Digital Business Transformation, 2019

You get the drift. The guiding objectives of a transformation pertain to a single line of business, but the relevant people, data, and infrastructure are almost always spread all over the company. To turn this idea of instruments as organizational resources into something executable, and meaningful to the question of how to transform, consider the following flow of a transformation program (see Figure 23).

Fig. 23: **How Instruments Factor into Orchestration**

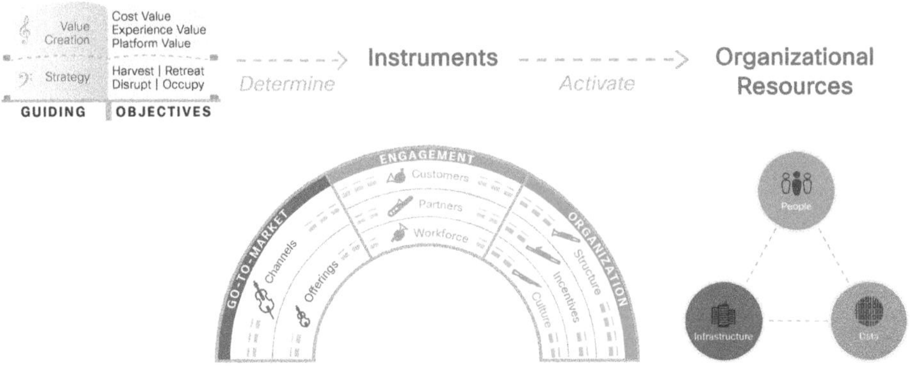

Source: Global Center for Digital Business Transformation, 2019

As we explained in the previous chapter, the company sets guiding objectives, including how it will create value for customers, how it will operationalize and monetize those efforts with the right business models, and the portfolio of strategies it will execute across its different lines of business. In other words, it composes the symphony to be played, its sheet music. From there, various transformation challenges emerge—problems that reflect a deficiency in a capability that's needed to achieve the guiding objectives.

A transformation challenge dictates which instruments must be played when addressing the problem. These instruments are made up of the three types of organizational resources—people, data, and infrastructure—linked in their support of a specific business need, such as changing the culture or workforce engagement.

Returning to our friends at BikeCo, you'll recall that the company is pursuing a Disrupt strategy with a new platform-based marketplace, BikeCo SHIFT, for its bicycle components business. Figure 24 depicts BikeCo's organizational chart, showing all the major functions and their respective teams. The orange boxes highlight all the "people resources" the company needs to build its platform.

You can clearly see that these resources span the entire organization. Digital business transformation has little hope of succeeding when it takes a function-specific approach because many of the necessary resources get excluded. This view represents just people, but the same holds true for BikeCo's other organizational resources: its data and infrastructure.

Fig. 24: People Resources Needed for BikeCo's Platform Business

Source: *Global Center for Digital Business Transformation, 2019*

PLAYING IN HARMONY

As shown in Figure 25, executives recognize the need for resources to work in harmony. But getting them to do so—to execute together—is a different matter. Achieving this connectedness among resources is both important and problematic.

Fig. 25: The Importance and Challenge of Connecting Organizational Resources

Survey Q. To what extent is lack of connectedness (e.g., between people, data, assets) in your organization a challenge to transformation?

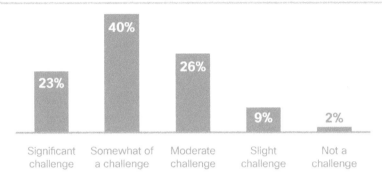

Survey Q. To accomplish a successful transformation initiative in your organization, how important is it to connect resources (e.g., people, data, assets) across multiple groups (e.g., departments, business units)?

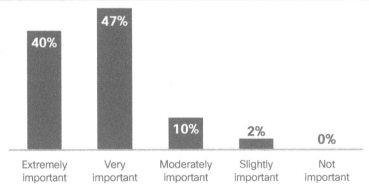

N=1,030

Source: Global Center for Digital Business Transformation, 2019

Cisco's Nina Lualdi, vice president of business model evolution, makes plain the frustration companies feel in achieving connectedness among resources across the value chain: "The problem was the functions were not necessarily interlocking well. It wasn't that they didn't understand they need to interlock. They did. But the environment that we had didn't allow them to interlock in a way that creates action, that resolves issues. Execution was held hostage."

Organizational resources must work together in a transformation. If any resources are not aligned, not doing their job, or are executing in an "off key" way, the transformation effort will be derailed. In short, everything and everybody must work together.

In many math and science disciplines there's something known as the "Anna Karenina principle." This principle describes situations in which a deficiency in any one area dooms the entire endeavor to failure. The name comes from the opening lines of Leo Tolstoy's master work: "All happy families are alike; each unhappy family is unhappy in its own way." By this, Tolstoy meant that every couple that is happy in their marriage has successfully navigated *all* the conditions necessary for happiness: love, fidelity, financial security, compatibility of personality, shared values, and so forth. All these factors must be working properly for the marriage to be happy. By contrast, there are many *different* ways for couples to be *un*happy. A big problem in even one area is likely to undermine marital bliss.

This is why the concept of instruments is so crucial. It gets transformation practitioners thinking holistically about the resources that are necessary—and that must work harmoniously—to achieve the organization's aims.

This does not imply the need for perfection, but rather that an array of factors contributes to the success or failure of any undertaking. So it is with organizational resources in the context of company transformations.

As Roel Louwhoff, chief transformation officer and COO of Netherlands-based financial services provider ING, explained in our conversation, "Every element is important and will need to deliver, because if one of the components doesn't, you basically can't deliver on the end-to-end promise." A major deficiency in one resource area leads to an organizational "trophic cascade" like the one caused by the reintroduction of gray wolves to Yellowstone National Park, where effects ripple across the system. The whole exercise of transformation can be brought down by gaps or shortcomings in any one area. If you lack the right people or the right data or the right infrastructure, the whole effort can collapse on itself.

This is why the concept of instruments is so crucial. It gets transformation practitioners thinking holistically about the resources that are necessary—and that must work harmoniously—to achieve the organization's aims. Even if a company comprises thousands of different people, data, and infrastructure resources, the eight instruments of the Transformation Orchestra let us conceive of these resources in a simplified yet comprehensive way—one that isn't restricted by a conventional, function-oriented mindset.

BACK TO BIKECO ...

After a thorough analysis of the market, BikeCo's leadership recognized an opportunity to extend its value proposition by developing a new platform: an online marketplace for bicycle components. By focusing on this marketplace concept, a clear transformation challenge emerges: how to build and operate a successful digital platform to connect BikeCo and other stakeholders to end customers. This challenge was not trivial. As a manufacturer and retailer, BikeCo had no experience building or operating digital platforms.

The Transformation Orchestra frames the challenge in terms of how to build a solution. BikeCo executives identified three instruments that were the biggest priorities: Offerings, Channels, and Partner Engagement. First, the platform is an entirely new type of offering and needs to be developed. Second, the traditional channel relationships—manufacturer, retailer, and consumer—will be disrupted by the online marketplace. Finally, BikeCo will need to create an ecosystem of partners to populate the marketplace. The company can't do it alone.

BikeCo's platform challenge has been identified and broken down into major elements (instruments). Now, the company is ready for the execution phase. Here, it needs to examine the mix of people, data, and infrastructure required to address the challenge.

It's at this stage that transformation becomes quite tactical. Building a platform-based marketplace will require people from multiple departments and functions, including internal IT, external IT vendors, product marketing, channel marketing, legal, supply chain, finance, and HR. Some of these roles already exist. Others do not, and will need to be hired or contracted. Various forms of data will need to be collected and managed. Finally, hardware and software infrastructure to support the marketplace will need to be acquired or developed.

A transformation network is the orchestration of organizational resources from multiple instruments in a way that addresses a particular transformation challenge.
Process changes and better capabilities (i.e., new ways of doing things) are the outputs of transformation networks.

For the purpose of illustration, let's focus on just one instrument: BikeCo's offerings. In the past, the company had no offerings with platform characteristics. All the money it ever made from bicycle components came from selling parts that went directly from a BikeCo retail outlet (or warehouse, if it was a catalog or online purchase) or from a distribution partner (an independent bike shop or retail chain) to the end customer. Now, the company wants to disrupt the market by reintermediating commerce and creating a new way of transacting.

Let's apply the transformation flow described earlier to BikeCo's situation (see Figure 26). A Disrupt strategy focused on platform value means that three instruments are the priority: Offerings, Channels, and Partner Engagement. (For simplicity's sake, Figure 26 shows only the *Offerings*-related details. However, a variety of organizational resources, including people, data, and infrastructure from multiple instruments, would be needed to create BikeCo's platform.)

Fig. 26: **From Guiding Objectives to Resource Orchestration**

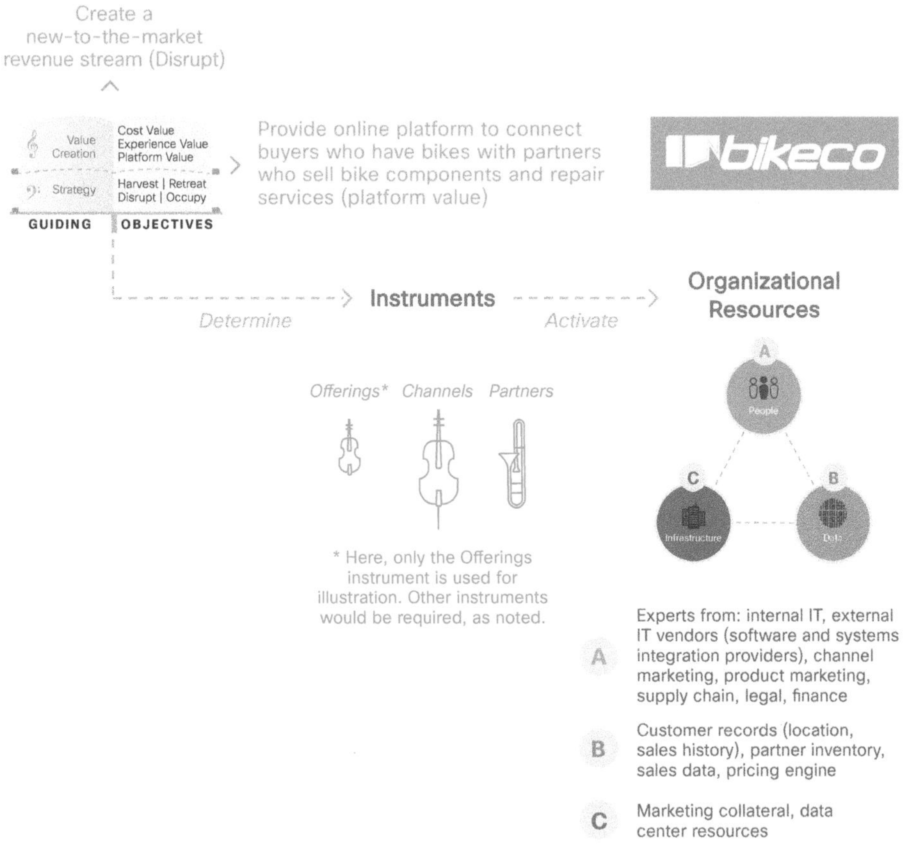

Create a
new-to-the-market
revenue stream (Disrupt)

	Cost Value
Value Creation	Experience Value
	Platform Value
Strategy	Harvest | Retreat
	Disrupt | Occupy

GUIDING | **OBJECTIVES**

Provide online platform to connect buyers who have bikes with partners who sell bike components and repair services (platform value)

bikeco

Instruments

Determine   Activate

Organizational Resources

Offerings* *Channels* *Partners*

* Here, only the Offerings instrument is used for illustration. Other instruments would be required, as noted.

A   People

C   Infrastructure   B   Data

A   Experts from: internal IT, external IT vendors (software and systems integration providers), channel marketing, product marketing, supply chain, legal, finance

B   Customer records (location, sales history), partner inventory, sales data, pricing engine

C   Marketing collateral, data center resources

Source: Global Center for Digital Business Transformation, 2019

How do you decide which instruments to focus on?

For BikeCo, Offerings, Channels, and Partner Engagement were considered the critical instruments for building a new platform business model. Focusing on too many instruments (or all the instruments) simultaneously doesn't really help. In our experience, this approach inevitably leads to poor outcomes, just as if all instruments in an orchestra started to play at once.

Some instruments are quite complementary. For example, if you want to launch a new product, this will probably involve resources from the Offerings, Channels, and Customer Engagement instruments. If you want to address talent, you probably want to address Workforce Engagement, Culture, and Incentives. These are natural pairings.

However, your organization will need to "conduct" the orchestra in a way that suits its own guiding objectives. How do you determine which instruments go together? That will depend on the symphony you compose.

Let's look at this in more detail.

TRANSFORMATION NETWORKS

Instruments help you move past narrow functional considerations when thinking about organizational resources. However, it's important to note that addressing any one instrument by itself is necessary, but insufficient, for successfully addressing a substantial transformation challenge, such as BikeCo's launch of a new platform.

Conceiving of organizational resources in a post-functional way and embracing a networked model for execution are the core of what it means to operate in the Orchestration Zone and to take a connected approach to change.

Instead, you must both mobilize and enable instruments to achieve a desired effect. In short, you need to orchestrate them. And when you orchestrate *multiple instruments,* a **transformation network** is formed.

The Transformation Orchestra and the notion of instruments help you *think* about the organization's resources. They represent a new mental model.

Transformation networks allow you to *execute* change differently. They represent a new model for execution. Conceiving of organizational resources in a post-functional way and embracing a networked model for execution are the core of what it means to operate in the Orchestration Zone and to take a connected approach to change.

A transformation network is the orchestration of organizational resources from multiple instruments in a way that addresses a particular transformation challenge. It merges people, data, and infrastructure from multiple instruments so that the challenge can be dealt with holistically. Together, these resources enable you to achieve a goal set by the organization's guiding objectives.

A transformation network should be small, focused, and empowered (we'll discuss how to do this in the next chapter), comprising resources drawn from between two and four instruments (more than this and the transformation network becomes too large and unwieldy to execute a specific change). The resources involved don't have a new reporting structure; they remain where they are in the business. But they work as a virtual structure to address the transformation challenge. When a transformation network does its job, the company will define and operate a new way of doing something. Process changes and better capabilities are, therefore, the outputs of transformation networks.

If and when the specified transformation challenge has been surmounted, these resources may continue to work together across the business to address related issues and sustain the change. Or, they can be "released" to work on other priorities. In some cases, the resources used to transform are themselves transformed in the bargain.

BikeCo, in its efforts to build and operate a new digital platform, cannot look at this challenge purely through the lens of offerings; channels and partner engagement are also crucial to successful execution. In a more linear world, BikeCo could pursue a serial "hip bone's connected to the thigh bone, thigh bone's connected to the knee

A transformation network is used to address challenges pertaining to the guiding objectives of one line of business. *Multiple transformation networks are needed to address the whole transformation, represented by the overall transformation ambition.*

bone" approach to addressing a big challenge like a new platform business. In the Orchestration Zone, all these instruments must be orchestrated in tandem.

Figure 27 shows that for BikeCo to successfully create a new plat-form-based business, it needs to combine people resources (shown in green) not just from the Offerings instrument, but also from Channels and Partner Engagement. This representation of the people needed for BikeCo's platform business is very different from the stovepipe resource view we saw in Figure 24. We can then incorporate other organizational resources, namely data and infrastructure-oriented re-sources (shown in gray and blue, respectively). Together, this gives us a complete picture of the resources BikeCo actually needs to create the platform.

Fig. 27: Transformation Network for BikeCo's Platform Business

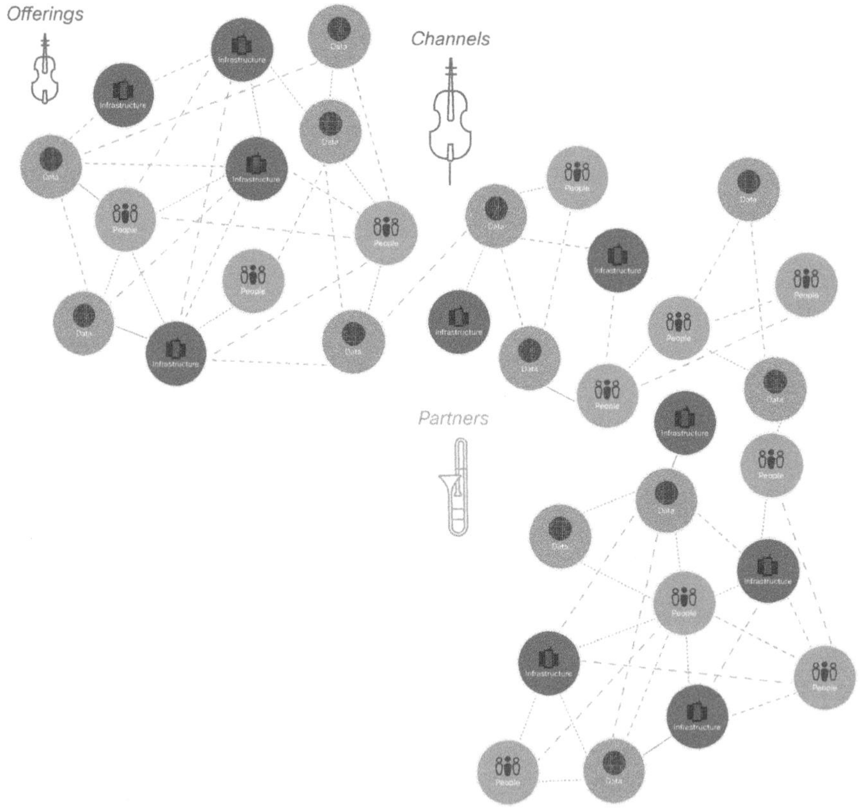

Source: Global Center for Digital Business Transformation, 2019

How is this different from what is normally seen in companies?

In the past, company bosses at BikeCo would have likely allocated funding for a platform, and then told someone (or a few people) to get to work on it. This work stream would create a lot of duplication, spending on purpose-built assets, and a whole team (maybe a new org structure or business unit). All of these are disconnected resources that are unlikely to create platform value in an integrated way or deliver much synergy.

Creating synergy is what transformation networks are all about. Transformation networks mobilize resources and enable them to work together. As Tricia Blair, CDO of $10 billion British professional services firm Aon plc, told us in our conversation: "Ultimately, in order for us to truly become a digital company, all of our resources have to work in congruence and in partnership."

Chances are BikeCo's platform leaders would not have planned for the reciprocally interdependent effects of creating a platform business inside the company at all. The joined-up approach of a transformation network, by contrast, permits the kind of managerial coordination we said earlier is associated with reciprocal interdependence (but which no one has known how to do): mutual adjustment.

An orchestrator does not "own" all the resources that he or she orchestrates, but rather puts the resources together (mobilizes) and enables them to work together optimally. And the orchestrator doesn't do all the work of transforming. That's what the resources are for—to accomplish the change.

Most large and midsized companies will have to tackle *multiple* transformation challenges at the same time, and they may have lots of capability deficiencies, not just one. Several transformation networks can be established to address these capability gaps, like a medley that represents several musical pieces that are successive or overlapping. At this point, the organization can combine all its transformation networks to form an end-to-end view of its resources and how they must work together to deliver synergistic execution in a comprehensive, integrated way (see Figure 28). This view allows you to identify resource overlaps, dependencies, and gaps, and to prioritize invest-

Less Is More

Many transformation programs are plagued by poorly defined ends and scope. Executing change via transformation networks, however, clearly delimits the aim and scope of a given change. Instead of transforming everything under the sun, a transformation network is geared to a given transformation challenge.
It has a very specific job to do: close the capability gap presented by the challenge and introduce a new process that allows the company to do something differently. Having a roadmap comprising a small number of transformation networks makes orchestration more manageable.

Many of the practitioners we met stressed the importance of taking a "pragmatic" approach to transformation. First and foremost, this involves a small number of well-defined activities that tackle the transformation challenge from end to end. As Cisco COO Irving Tan told us, "I would rather have four or five really strategic things—things that are truly material to the business, digitized from end to end—than to

(Continued on next page)

ment. Some resources may be needed to address multiple challenges and, therefore, will play a role in more than one transformation network.

For BikeCo, not only did its transformation ambition of "50 in 4 by 25" (50 percent of revenues coming from online channels in all four lines of business by 2025) call for (1) a platform-based business model in its components business, it also necessitated (2) attracting new digital talent to the firm, and (3) creating an innovation ecosystem in its other businesses.

A transformation network is used to address challenges pertaining to the guiding objectives of *one* line of business. *Multiple* transformation networks are needed to address the whole transformation, represented by the overall transformation ambition.

BikeCo can also connect to the organizational resources of *other* firms, such as suppliers and retailers (shown in red and purple in Figure 28).

This will help it address higher-order transformation challenges that involve multiparty orchestration, such as ecosystem creation. Many business models require orchestration outside the four walls of the business. Platforms, ecosystems, communities, and crowds can all be orchestrated using this approach.

When we marry transformation networks in this way, something really powerful comes into view: the company's executable digital transformation roadmap. This "network of networks" approach is a very different take on the idea of a roadmap. There is a map, but no road! Roadmaps, as we've known them in the past, are far too linear for the Orchestration Zone.

The network of networks represents all the change that has to happen to realize the company's overall transformation ambition. If it's successful in producing new processes and better capabilities through its transformation networks, the company is well positioned to achieve this ambition.

The approach we're advocating is neither a serial project plan nor an agenda so grandiose that no one knows how to execute it. There's no "boiling the ocean" here (see sidebar "Less Is More"). Instead, it allows the company to pursue a series of smaller, targeted, and achievable outcomes that link together to produce synergy (e.g., economies of scale, learning, operating efficiencies) that benefits execution on all fronts.

Orchestration is the *connecting of organizational resources in a synergistic way*—mobilizing and enabling them so as to achieve a desired effect. While the resources you are connecting are obviously valuable, they're just half of the equation. The other half, the *connections,* play just as big a role. "We're basically bringing together and connecting the dots in digital. The value you get from digital is from the connections, from the synergies," explained Jessica Federer, former CDO at $40 billion German pharmaceutical leader Bayer.[3]

Less Is More

(Continued from previous page)

have a hundred things 'a little bit digital.'"

Randstad North America CDO Alan Stukalsky put it this way: "Minimize the volume of parts of the initiative. Don't do 10 things fairly well when you can do five things great. Get really, really good at those five things so that you achieve high utilization and focus the people. There's only so much change that the audience can really take at one time, and if you try to throw too much at them, you're not going to be successful in anything. That's definitely one of the big lessons learned that we've had."

Fig. 28: **Combining Transformation Networks**

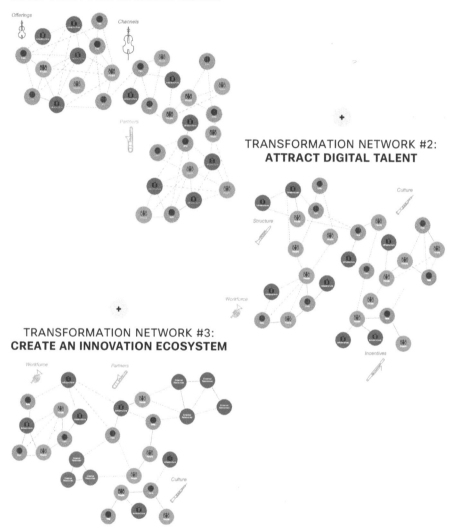

TRANSFORMATION NETWORK #1:
BUILD PLATFORM BUSINESS MODEL

TRANSFORMATION NETWORK #2:
ATTRACT DIGITAL TALENT

TRANSFORMATION NETWORK #3:
CREATE AN INNOVATION ECOSYSTEM

Source: Global Center for Digital Business Transformation, 2019

WHAT IS A NETWORK?

Networks are hardly a new concept in organizational theory. Networks play an important role in virtually all fields where organizations come under the microscope, including psychology, sociology, political science, economics, industrial and labor relations, management, and law.

As we turn to the mechanics of executing organizational change, and how companies can operationalize the concept of transformation networks, let's step back for a minute. Let's explore a simple, but important, question: what *is* a network?

Generally, people think of a network as a web of things that are connected somehow. In the 20th century, a telephony network was made up of telephones that connected over wires, through a central exchange, and then over still more wires to other telephones (and to the people who talked on those phones).

To think about transformation in a networked way, let's say that networks are, at their most basic, made up of *nodes* and *connections.* In our telephony example, the phones can be thought of as nodes, and the wires are the connections. Telephones aren't very useful if there are no wires to carry voice signals (i.e., if the nodes aren't connected).

In the context of a transformation network, the nodes are the company's resources, meaning its people, data, and infrastructure.

And the connections? What are they? They are the relationships and activities that take place *between* nodes. The connections can be

> When resources have access to new or relevant information *and* they operate with trust and cohesion, the organization is much better positioned to tackle the transformation dilemma. Information flowing among connected resources is what counteracts organizational entanglement.

between humans, between humans and machines, and between machines, all of which constitute organizational resources. Communications, information sharing, processes, workflows, collaboration, engagement, transactions—these are all forms of interaction that occur due to these relationships, traveling over the connections between nodes.

Those old telephones, even if they were functioning just fine themselves, would also not be very useful if the voice quality was so poor that you couldn't hear your grandmother on the other end of the line. In other words, the connections have to work well.

In a digital transformation, the connections among resources also have to work well—to produce synergy.

THE WEAK AND THE STRONG

To better understand what connections are, and the role they play in orchestration, let's consider one of the most prominent disciplines within network theory: social network analysis (SNA). In 1973, American sociologist Mark Granovetter published "The Strength of Weak Ties," which would become the most widely cited sociology article of all time and serve as a cornerstone in the development of SNA and some of the world's best-known social media.[4]

Granovetter's "ties" are what we would call "connections." They are the relationships between nodes in a network. Weak connections occur when there is no strong linkage or relationship. The strength of a connection between two nodes can be measured by the frequency of their interaction, the ability and willingness to share or collaborate between the two nodes, and the level of affinity between the two nodes.[5] We have weak connections with people we don't know well or with whom we rarely interact.

Granovetter maintained that weak connections are actually very potent. This is because they act, in his terminology, as "bridges" that transmit *new or relevant information* between network nodes.

Consider a job seeker. A person with a lot of weak connections has a better chance to hear about a good job through his or her network than someone with a smaller, more tightly bound network of close colleagues. This is because the first job seeker can pick up the vibrations from farther out across his or her network to access this valuable information. If you use LinkedIn for professional networking, you're probably familiar with this phenomenon and how it works (i.e., second- and third-level "connections"). A network that includes a lot of weak connections means that more nodes can be reached.

Weak connections are extremely valuable in the context of transformation. They allow us to connect highly distributed resources so they can interact, collaborate, and share new or relevant information to address a particular challenge, even if they are far-flung geographically or organizationally.

As valuable as new or relevant information may be, however, we also want *strong connections* among organizational resources, especially people. Strong connections are what create *trust and cohesion* in relationships—two factors that play a huge role in organizational change. As SNA researcher David Krackhardt notes, "People resist change and are uncomfortable with uncertainty. Strong ties constitute a base of trust that can reduce resistance and provide comfort in the face of uncertainty."[6]

In our interview, Matthew Friedman, CDO at the $6 billion Singaporean utilities, marine, and urban development group Sembcorp, reflected on the importance of strong connections among employees when driving change: "Not many things get done without people, trust, and relationships. And it takes time to build those things. Don't think that just because you have focused on delivering projects, that means you have the confidence, trust, and support of the colleagues you need with you to be successful."

Although SNA is concerned mainly with people relationships, other organizational resources have relationships, too. The strength of connections between data sources is measured by the level of information exchange. The strength of connections between two infrastructure assets is measured by the level of integration and interoperability. In other words, how effectively can these resources "talk" to one another?

Ultimately, organizations need a large number of weak connections *and* a smaller number of strong connections to drive change quickly and effectively. They need the new or relevant information (and access to disparate resources) that a web of weak connections provides. They depend on the trust and cohesion of strong connections to ensure that the resources work together effectively. Transformation networks need this trust and cohesion because they represent resources from different parts of the business that may not have a natural kinship, or any previous contact for that matter, despite both resources having a role to play in tackling a particular challenge.

Think about the difference between the spreading of a rumor and the keeping of a secret. A rumor can be transmitted rapidly to a large group of people over a distributed web of relationships, among people who may have only a passing acquaintance (i.e., weak connections). This information can have a huge impact on a large number of people in a very short period. Information that "goes viral" is disseminated in this way.

A secret is something that can be held tightly between two close friends. This information is not transmitted widely. In fact, its confidentiality is based on the closeness of the relationship. The two friends, who have a strong connection, are bound together as a unit. The impact of keeping that secret can profoundly deepen that relationship.

Spreading rumors and keeping secrets are not necessarily healthy for organizations. (That's certainly not the point we're making.) But the ways that rumors are spread and secrets are kept reflect the value in both types of connections. There's value in the ability to transmit new or relevant information through weak connections. There's value in the trust and cohesion that come from strong connections. When resources have access to new or relevant information *and* they operate with trust and cohesion, the organization is much better positioned to tackle the transformation dilemma. Information flowing among connected resources is what counteracts organizational entanglement.

CHAPTER 5
Orchestration Competencies

FROM ORGANIC TO ORCHESTRATED

At $22 billion American electronics manufacturing services provider Jabil, the engineers have long believed that change (finding new ways of doing things) is their day-to-day responsibility. "There were pockets within the company where you had talented engineers starting to conduct their own designer experiments and really doing a lot of skunkworks–like downloading open source AI algorithms and applying them to problems they were seeing," said Dan Gamota, vice president of digital services. This was happening all over the company, across multiple divisions, among thousands of engineers, all of whom were using digital in numerous, mostly uncoordinated ways to make changes in how the business operated.

Today, added Gamota, "everything has evolved from the fragmented, highly entrepreneurial, creative, innovative but not cohesively brought together approach to the formal orchestration of ways to deploy appropriately the most robust and scalable solutions. I think that's the evolution–from organic to orchestrated."

One CDO with whom we met described the issue this way: "Anyone could do anything 'digital' without triggering any awareness. They could build a website with a digital agency, or do a machine learning pilot in Bolivia without anyone knowing, as long as they didn't exceed a finance threshold of $150,000." Today, his firm's "digital lab" approach–in which the CDO and his team furnish innovation and proof-of-concept resources to the business to incent stakeholders to coordinate digital initiatives–aims to reduce the patchwork of "shadow digital" efforts occurring across the company.

Unfortunately, our research indicates that cases like these are not common. At most companies, the orchestrated management of resources across the business remains an elusive goal (see Figure 29).

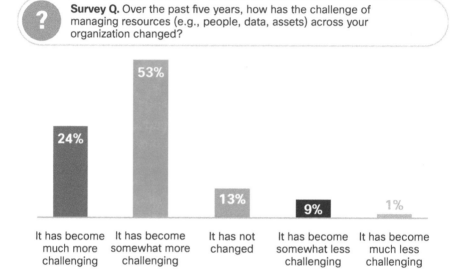

Fig. 29: **Managing Resources Across the Business Is a Major Challenge**

Survey Q. Over the past five years, how has the challenge of managing resources (e.g., people, data, assets) across your organization changed?

53%

24%

13%

9%

1%

It has become much more challenging | It has become somewhat more challenging | It has not changed | It has become somewhat less challenging | It has become much less challenging

N=1,030

Source: Global Center for Digital Business Transformation, 2019

As leaders, most of our efforts focus on improving the performance of individual resources. This management approach even has a name: "resource optimization." For a lot of managers, that's their job—getting the most out of a given resource.

That's not good enough for the Orchestration Zone and digital business transformation. Here, we must focus our efforts on solving for *connectedness.*

Figure 30 shows eight **orchestration competencies** that companies should possess to mobilize resources and enable the connections between them. These competencies are all replicable, real-world examples of how practitioners are propelling their organizations with a more connected approach to change. Let's review these next.

Fig. 30: **Orchestration Competencies**

MOBILIZE RESOURCES

Bridge from Guiding Objectives
1. Customer journey mapping
2. Business model design

Understand the State of the Organization
3. Business architecture
4. Capability assessment

ENABLE CONNECTIONS

Build Synergy
5. Communications and training
6. Incubation and scaling platforms

Accelerate the Transformation
7. Internal venture funding
8. Agile ways of working

Source: Global Center for Digital Business Transformation, 2019

BRIDGE FROM GUIDING OBJECTIVES

Organizations can't follow the "fire, ready, aim" approach to transformation. They need to link the guiding objectives to their transformation program's structure in order to execute change, much as Intuit did (see Chapter 3). Customer value creation, business models, and strategy have to be front and center.

What do you need to bridge guiding objectives and execution?

(1) Customer journey mapping is a needed competency. For example, at Coats, a $1.5 billion UK-headquartered textile supplies manufacturer, "rather than trying to start our transformation in different places, we wanted to start with customers," said Hizmy Hassen, chief digital and technology officer. "That gave us a real understanding of how digital would transform how customers engage with us and how that creates the opportunity to transform our competitive advantage."

Because of the central role that customer value creation plays in setting guiding objectives, it's vital to understand what the customer values. This involves moment-of-truth analysis, charting of customer pain points, competitive analysis, and value engineering.

Many of our interviewees emphasized the impact of the customer journey on the execution of a transformation program, as well as the need for a strong competency in its mapping and analysis. Said Cynthia Stoddard, CIO of $7 billion American software maker Adobe, "You need to continually look at yourself and be innovative, and say, 'How do I connect with the consumer better? How do I make their journey smoother?' And look across the different points of the journey and say, 'How do we take out any friction points?' or maybe even 'How do we add value that customers might not even know they want yet?'"

Ryan Ostrom, CDO at KFC, a division of the US-based quick-service restaurant conglomerate Yum! Brands, commented that the customer journey becomes an anchoring point for connecting multiple transformation efforts: "When you look at traditionally how organizations were structured ... they have the traditional IT arm, they have the traditional marketing arm. You need someone in between who understands the customer but also understands the technical side and how you bring those two worlds together to really optimize the customer journey."

Customer journey mapping means achieving a detailed understanding of customers' experiences from the beginning to the end of their interactions with an organization. The proliferation of digital channels is changing how companies approach this mapping.

Consider today's typical multichannel retailer. Shopper interactions once comprised a small handful of possible journeys. But taking into account new channels, including mobile, online, wearables, and in-home devices (e.g., Amazon Echo), we've calculated that today's shoppers have more than 800 unique variations of possible shopping journeys.[1]

In an interview with our team, Cyril Lamblard, head of e-business and digital marketing at Nespresso, the coffee brand of the $91 billion Swiss consumer goods giant Nestlé SA, described the steps his company has taken to map and redefine the customer journey across its multiple channels. Nespresso has focused its efforts on providing the best experience to its customers in a channel-agnostic fashion. For Lamblard, the job is to "deliver consistent and relevant customer experiences wherever the customer is"—whether that's in a physical store or an online channel. Nespresso maps pain points during the customer journey at a micro level, making it as frictionless as possible and driving harmonization among channels.

Toward that end, Lamblard and his digital team gather all complaints from digital customers worldwide, as do all channel leaders. They capture complaints every week, then filter them, group them, and analyze them to identify the main friction points along the customer journey. According to Lamblard, "We know where we are suffering on a weekly basis." This allows Nespresso to adjust its journey-optimization priorities according to the reality of the customers' experiences.

Lamblard suggested that e-commerce and user experience (UX) will increasingly focus on removing friction points across the customer journey. "The future of UX is no UX," he said, and "e-commerce checkouts will vanish." To accomplish this omnichannel reality, Nespresso aims to eliminate all unnecessary steps from the customer journey by leveraging data and personalization at scale. (For example, when future customers shop in a boutique, they will simply choose their coffee and then leave.) Examples of digital capabilities that may facilitate this seamless journey include subscription ordering models, AI, automation, and peer-to-peer commerce.

Nespresso has motivated its channels to work together by harmonizing cross-channel employee incentives. (This makes the company not only a prime example of customer journey mapping, but of orchestration that combines multiple "instruments".)

For example, when Nespresso wanted to promote its mobile channel, it had trouble motivating workers in its 700+ boutiques worldwide. Front-line employees were afraid that mobile sales would cannibalize in-boutique sales. To tackle the problem, Nespresso decided to measure its boutique employees on *all* sales within a particular catchment area (geographic region) instead of only on what was purchased in a physical store. In this way, Nespresso is making sure that employees push all channels. In-store employees are using tablets to register customers and promote mobile and e-commerce channels. At the same time, Nespresso can refer customers to boutiques through its online channels. The result? Customers enjoy a seamless journey through the channel that best suits their needs.

For most incumbents, this is the kind of thorough approach that customer journey mapping requires. "It's really all about that customer journey and not silo-ing it within a specific channel, realizing that the customer is the single focus of everything that you do, no matter where they decide to interact with you," said Rob Roy, CDO at Sprint, the $32 billion American telecommunications provider.

(2) Business model design is a complementary competency. Key to business model reinvention is a keen understanding of customers' expectations and what they'll pay for. Management consulting skills in strategy and business modeling (e.g., the Business Model Canvas) are important here, as is an understanding of customer value creation. How are other firms—especially disruptive competitors—creating cost value, experience value, and/or platform value for customers?

Competitive intelligence also plays a big role in understanding how the market is evolving. Orchestrators can help the executive leadership team (and others responsible for setting guiding objectives) understand how competitors are redefining value in the industry, and what forms of value the company should build into its offerings.

Frithjof Netzer, CDO at German chemicals giant BASF SE, described what this looks like in his organization:

> I have seasoned business people in digital business models, and they have a special skill set, a methodology that they can bring to workshops in which the high level of innovativeness is exclusively targeting top-line growth. They will be able to take groups of people with industry-specific domain expertise, combine them with people with no industry expertise in that field and then, as a stimulant, facilitate these teams, drive them toward executable validated business ideas and within months, as a follow up, create a minimum viable product.

Design thinking is a related discipline that practitioners increasingly rely on to address truly "wicked problems," such as the disruptive dynamics of the Digital Vortex and the complex challenge of organizational entanglement.[2] This approach, which is used by many of the companies we've studied, can be applied to customer journey mapping *and* business model design. Aon plc's CDO Tricia Blair told us, "The creation of a center of excellence around design thinking and user experience has definitely been a critical construct for us to evolve and develop."

We recommend training a small number of people in design thinking so they can engage others inside and outside the business in "solutioning"—understanding the problem or opportunity and what the affected people (customers, salespeople, engineers) truly value. These design thinkers can also facilitate brainstorming, rapid prototyping, and iterative design.

Customer journey mapping and business model design also require value modeling skills—the ability to create use cases and value logic to quantify business outcomes and the financial impacts of a transformation program. Value modeling is vital for effectively tracking progress and creating clarity and buy-in across the organization. A small team of financial analysts, with strong modeling and outside-the-box quantification skills, can "size the prize" of value vacancies or unearth hidden caches of value trapped in the organization.

They should spend their time calculating the total addressable market for new businesses and the net present value of future cash flows associated with transformation investments. These resources can help dimension the costs and benefits of defined transformation initiatives, and quantify new opportunities and risks that can aid in setting the guiding objectives themselves. Establishing metrics for transformation networks can be another important activity (see sidebar, "Made to Measure").

A note of caution: although measurement and value modeling are important for keeping transformation programs on track, financial strictures can sometimes put the brakes on innovative activities whose returns may not be felt for years. As Matt Anderson, CDO and president of $27 billion American electronic components and computer services distributor Arrow Electronics, said, "In many ways, I think the business case process is an artifact of a culture that tends to suppress and kill innovation."

Many companies we encounter aren't very good at measuring what they do. It's not a muscle they've developed over the years. For this reason (in part), we recommend—as a key orchestration competency—hiring a small cadre of financial analysts to conduct value modeling of your transformation efforts. Being able to quantify the benefits of change, and measure progress toward the goal, is immensely helpful.

Made to Measure

A common question we get from executives is, "How do we measure success?" That's a hard one. The variety of transformation ambitions, guiding objectives, and the resulting transformation challenges is nearly infinite.

A company's transformation ambition should include an element of measurability (the "M" in our "PRISM" framework). This will tell everybody about the state of the company's competitiveness, such as how much business comes from outside the country where it's headquartered or the amount of money the company realizes from digital channels.

Many transformation programs are perceived as failures because they're simply not conducive to measurement. Many have "soft" goals such as changing the company culture or increasing innovation. Putting a dollar value on such nebulous aspirations is an exercise in quantifying the unquantifiable.

Because process change and better capabilities are the outputs of transformation networks, metrics should focus

(Continued on next page)

The late Intel CEO Andy Grove's adage that "you can't manage what you don't measure" goes to the core of succeeding at digital business transformation.

Value modeling depends on measurement, but it's not synonymous with it. Instead, value modelling is about capturing and using data to estimate business outcomes.

New customers acquired is a *measurement*. Incremental revenue from new customers is a business *outcome*. Business outcomes may include market share gains, revenue uplift, cost savings, and so forth. These are concrete developments that contribute to competitiveness and shareholder value.

UNDERSTAND THE STATE OF THE ORGANIZATION

(3) Business architecture is a competency that helps orchestrators to mobilize organizational resources and assemble transformation networks.

The Open Group, a global technology standards-setting consortium, defines business architecture as "a description of the structure and interaction between the business strategy, organization, functions, business processes, and information needs."[3] For our purposes, "business architecture" refers to a competency in mapping the company's nodes and connections—its resources and their relationships.[4]

When mobilizing resources in transformation networks, companies must identify "who's who in the zoo" (which individuals and which teams do what), which data exists, and where different things (like computing resources or capital assets) sit, as well as their status. Imagine using a giant pen to draw a circle around all the people, data, and infrastructure relevant to a given instrument in the Transformation Orchestra. This lets you see which resources can be brought to bear when changes are needed. Once you catalog the pertinent resources, you know where your points of leverage are.

Cisco's Ashley Goodall, senior vice president of leadership and team intelligence, explained how mapping resources in this way was important to the transformation challenge he faced in the HR organization, which was ensuring that every Cisco team performed like the company's best teams:

> First, find all of the teams working within the organization. It sounds simple, but before we can make more teams like our best teams, we need to be able to locate all teams. If you look at the typical human resource information system (HRIS) or organization chart, you'll find a very dated representation of what's actually going on. This is because the system takes time to reflect the reality of teams as changes occur. More importantly, the representation is

Made to Measure

(Continued from previous page)

on "before and after" snapshots of a given process or capability. For example, "Before we made this change, our cost was $59 per service call. Afterward, it was $35." Remember to go slowly at first so you can set a "before" benchmark for the relevant processes and capabilities.

With transformation networks, we can say with precision which resources are involved in executing the change (and which are impacted by it). We can "chunk" execution into readily identifiable work streams involving a defined set of resources. Because the transformation network is for one line of business and one given challenge, modeling and measuring the process and capability changes is much more feasible—and straightforward.

When trying to understand a measure such as ROI, a common bad practice among incumbents is putting more focus on the "return" than the "investment." However, by clearly defining a transformation network, gauging the costs becomes easier.

actually incomplete because a lot of the work done is on project or cross-functional teams, or teams that cut across the boundaries in the org chart. Very few organizations, if any, have a technology platform that allows them to see all the different teams at any moment in time. The first thing we are doing at Cisco with our performance management technology is creating the ability to capture all of the teams. The technology will allow people to go into the system and create what we call "dynamic teams."[5]

Appyndix 2 provides a comprehensive list of illustrative organizational resources that make up each of the eight instruments of the Transformation Orchestra. You can use this as a thought starter for the kinds of resources your company has—resources relevant to a particular challenge.

Mapping organizational resources is important. It allows you to create clusters of "which instruments and resources matter" for a given challenge. Without this map, organizational entanglement makes change very hard to navigate. "As an architect, mapping is the location equivalent in the real estate world," said Suncor's Michael Loughlean. "Our digital focus areas, who's responsible for those capabilities, and where they exist in other places in the organization all need to be understood."

It's also wise to inventory every active digital project, as Ann-Christin Andersen did after assuming the CDO role at TechnipFMC. Documenting the current state of play creates awareness of where investment is being channeled and where it could be redirected. The goal is to achieve what Patrick Attallah, vice president of data analytics at $10 billion Dutch consumer and industrial goods giant DSM, calls a "drone-level view of the business." Although not its express purpose, this mapping may also identify waste, redundancy, and inefficiencies. In addition, it may illuminate capability gaps that indicate the presence of a previously unrecognized transformation challenge.

A lack of visibility into who is doing what can starve orchestration efforts of oxygen, creating duplication and undercutting possible synergies. Frithjof Netzer, CDO of BASF SE, noted that his group promotes visibility "by providing a joint digital cockpit in which all the digital projects—including their costs and benefit potential—are logged. They are logged in there for the purpose of providing a best-practice exchange." Using the digital cockpit tool, managers who are considering investments in projects can identify related work streams, their status, ownership, and other details.

The transformation challenges that companies face are a function of capability gaps in their organizational resources. If BikeCo wants to launch a platform business, does it have the resources to do it? In our Transformation Orchestra framework, it may find it doesn't have any "violinists" (or developers who know Python or Ruby), or that those it does have aren't skilled enough. If so, it needs to figure out how to put the right resources in place and get them working together.

Therefore, another necessary step in mobilizing organizational resources is *(4) capability assessment*, including the availability and readiness of resources. To do this, begin by answering the following questions:

- Do we have the right *people* to execute our strategies? Do they have the skills required to do the job? Where are the gaps, and how do we close them?

- Do we have the *data* we need to execute our strategies? Are we capturing, consolidating, and analyzing it effectively? Where are the gaps, and how do we close them?

- Do we have the right *infrastructure* to execute our strategies? What equipment, facilities, IT, and other assets are we missing? Where are the gaps, and how do we close them?

Figure 31 provides a basic capability assessment framework for organizational resources, with a five-stage maturity model ranging from nonexistent to expert. This helps you identify capability gaps among the instruments relevant to a set of guiding objectives. For BikeCo, the instruments most critical for its platform business were identified as Offerings, Channels, and Partner Engagement. Using this capability assessment framework, BikeCo determined where the big capability gaps were, and how it could prioritize its investment.

Fig. 31: Capability Assessment Framework

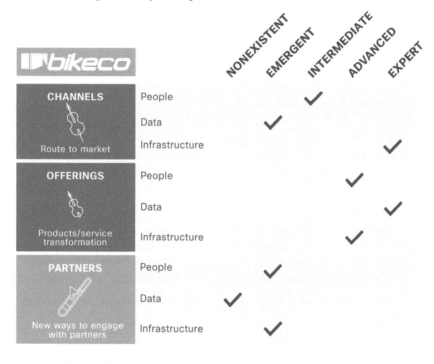

Source: Global Center for Digital Business Transformation, 2019

The output of this framework is not a substitute for an in-depth analysis of your organizational resources. Instead, you should consider it directional. Of course, every company has a different history and its own guiding objectives, so the resource gaps and paths to addressing them will differ for each. And because of the scope of transformation efforts in large and midsized companies, this assessment will involve a lot of legwork to get an accurate picture of which resources the company has—and doesn't yet have—at its disposal.

BUILD SYNERGY

Companies undergoing large-scale digital transformation are often places of confusion. A lack of both a clear vision and a shared narrative to describe the company's transformation efforts frequently prevents people from taking decisive action. For these reasons, *(5) communications and training* is a key orchestration competency.

Orchestrators can play a central role in developing and scaling a compelling narrative that conveys why the company must transform. This may include a description of the industry's dynamics, an examination of new, disruptive competitors, a picture of changing customer wants and needs, and the risks of failing to transform. The communications can help shape the transformation ambition, though it must be *set* at the executive level—it can't be one person's take on priorities and direction. The transformation ambition should be central to all organizational communications.

Once key stakeholders understand the business model evolution and its logic, the narrative must clearly explain the corresponding operating model changes, especially "what this means to you, the individual employee." This part of the narrative is critically important. The orchestrator needs to customize the story for specific audiences and objectives. He or she must then scale the narrative through mechanisms that include marketing communications programs, in-person events and workshops, training programs, and the media. Marketing departments, PR firms, executive communications personnel, investor and analyst relations teams, and learning and development organizations may also play a role in scaling the narrative.

> Appendix 3 provides a more complete table for capability assessment, covering all eight instruments of the Transformation Orchestra.

On top of this, orchestrators need specialized communications personnel who are focused on stakeholder management, including executive leadership, business partners (line-of-business and functional representatives), general employee communications, and partner communications. Their role is to drive stakeholder engagement for the transformation. This should include high-level reinforcement and explanation of the transformation ambition, the rationale and specifics of the business-level guiding objectives, and progress and status updates, including metrics.

A number of the practitioners we interviewed stressed how much time they spend "teaching." One CDO said, "You would not believe how much of my job is stakeholder education." This holds true for all levels of the business—from individual contributors, to the so-called "frozen middle," to the executive ranks. Teaching can occur as part of ongoing engagement with business partners or as formal training efforts on digital business or the transformation program and what it means for different groups.

Orchestrators should also provide *(6) incubation and scaling platforms.* Platforms are great for creating market change, and they are critical in driving organizational change as well. They are particularly useful in generating synergies and as scaling engines. As Jorn Lambert, executive vice president, digital solutions at $12.5 billion US financial services leader Mastercard, told us, new processes and better capabilities create value only when they can be leveraged at scale: "What I continually say to my team is, 'It's very easy to develop clever functionality and clever features. It's extremely hard to push it out at scale to our entire network of 23,000 banks. And so, unless you have a plan to get the features into 23,000 banks, I'm not interested.'"

Platforms can play an outsized role in enabling orchestration. They create scale through weak connections in which distributed resources collaborate with (or leverage) common tools and assets. Several companies we interviewed have built enabling platforms that allow their resources to collaborate and develop solutions at speed.

At $34 billion Swiss industrial giant ABB Group, a key enabler for driving change at scale is its innovative "ABB Ability" platform. It's a suite of compatible protocols and technologies that work in harmony across different products and services. CDO Guido Jouret explained how ABB Ability works.

"This is essentially software that allows our business units to build connected robots or connected motors more quickly, or to offer new digital services to our customers," he said. "My team basically scouts the technology landscape, looking for promising companies and their technology. We then procure them and make them available to our business units."

Another example is Adobe's DDOM (Data-Driven Operating Model) platform. "The goal is to enable the business and product teams to capitalize on data assets and drive insights and predictive analytics," said CIO Cynthia Stoddard. "With this enterprise-class data-driven operating model, we have integrated disparate big data at scale and we have aligned stakeholders across the company around a common language, consistent measurement, data governance, and actionable insights."

These internal platforms promote the cross-pollination across silos that orchestration requires. Randstad North America CDO Alan Stukalsky explained that, on a global basis, the company has built a "digital factory" that is "responsible for taking great ideas, great concepts and products that have been built in a single location, like the US or Mexico or Japan—a product or technology or process improvement that can 'travel'—and then packaging it in such a way that other countries can easily implement it so they don't have to build it from scratch."

A number of practitioners we interviewed stressed the role of data orchestration in creating synergy, using platforms such as a Hadoop cluster. "The foundation of any transformation has to be getting your arms wrapped around, aligning, and mastering data," said Thomson Reuters CDO Joe Miranda. This lets companies operationalize analytics and data-driven decisions in a connected way. Miranda noted, however, that a big challenge at Thomson Reuters, as with most large and midsized companies, was the usability of the data, which was "fragmented and messy," and not "orchestrated in a way in which people can look at it through dashboards" to gain insights or drive decision-making.

At Coats, the UK-headquartered maker of industrial threads, Chief Digital and Technology Officer Hizmy Hassen said, "A key insight for us has been provided by a data lake we created where we're able to bring in data from various applications and then blend it. That's starting to give us insights into the business, customer engagement, and how we run the supply chain that we haven't had before. Those insights are, therefore, driving different decisions, such as process reengineering, that we probably hadn't thought about previously."

ACCELERATE THE TRANSFORMATION

Consider a frequent scenario we've encountered, a kind of orchestration "false start." Picture a cross-functional tiger team that's been created to tackle a pressing transformation challenge. This group, supported by an expensive outside consultant, spends months assembling a plan to transform a series of key processes. The plan calls for resources from all over the company to take action to introduce a new way of doing something.

When things shift from planning mode to execution, however, the working group loses its mojo. The machine grinds to a halt because the business owners who control the resources on which the plan depends say, "That's an interesting plan you've come up with. Unfortunately, none of this work is in my budget for this fiscal year. I don't have the resources to do this and still meet my commitments. Sorry, my hands are tied."

Budgets, and the way they're created in large and midsized companies, are one of the biggest inhibitors of cross-functional execution, largely because they trail the state of the business. They are team-specific, highly linear, and essentially set in stone. And usually, there's little or no incentive (or leeway) to change them over the course of a quarter or a year. Budgets become excuse-makers—opt-out clauses that deprive the transformation effort of its lifeblood.

To solve this problem, some transformation practitioners have assumed the role of internal venture capitalist. In some cases, they have control over dedicated *(7) internal venture funding* focused on innovation and transformation.

As Frederic Herren, CDO of SGS, wryly remarked, "No one listens to a cost center. You've got to have financial means to be an attractive business partner." For a midsized company, this funding might run to a few million dollars. For a large global incumbent, it could be in the tens or even hundreds of millions of dollars. These funds should be ring-fenced for efforts that promote cross-functional outcomes.

ABB Group's digital transformation program was the brainchild of Ulrich Spiesshofer, who became CEO of the company in 2013. As part of the program, he created a CDO role, filled by Guido Jouret, who joined in 2016. The CDO organization within ABB was small, but also mighty. It possessed something that ABB stakeholders valued: funding.

An internal venture fund controlled by Jouret created incentives that promoted cross-functional outcomes among ABB's business units. Jouret used these funds to invest in transformation projects aligned to ABB organizational goals: "One of the ways I provide influence is with something we call 'lighthouse project' funding. I basically put funding behind collaboration incentives, meaning I tell [stakeholders] that I will fund projects where BUs work together, and when that happens, one plus one really does equal three." This approach spreads the financial burden for cross-functional outcomes among several stakeholders, eliminating a classic organizational "collective action dilemma," and unlocking execution.

Cisco offers another example of how a dedicated internal venture fund can surmount organizational division and accelerate a transformation program. During the 2015 planning process, the company's operations and digital transformation leaders realized that executing transformation initiatives beyond the departmental or functional level required a different approach. The issue? Because Cisco was facing major change across a highly entangled organization, it needed to work in the Orchestration Zone.

Provisioning, funding, and managing resources for major cross-functional change was proving highly complex. For example, how should leaders decide what contribution and effort each function should make, especially when the work takes place across functional silos toward a joint outcome that benefits the enterprise overall, but does not deliver results for each individual function? This issue often arises for transformation efforts aimed at improving enterprise-wide data quality, accelerating processes end-to-end across the value chain (e.g., automation across the entire quote-to-cash lifecycle), or building shared capabilities such as a center of excellence.

To address the issue, Cisco instituted a centralized fund called the Cisco Transformation Portfolio (CTP) that used a multi-tiered governance model. Sponsored by the executive leadership team, the CTP decision committee was made up of senior leaders from the functions, operations, and IT. It meets quarterly to make funding decisions.

This model introduced a centralized funding and prioritization mechanism at the senior leadership level. Endowed with a $100 million annual budget, it prioritizes cross-functional work streams based on their overall value and return, requiring that project sponsors validate the benefits and agree to include the value impact in their annual budgets. Groups from across Cisco can propose projects for CTP consideration in a "Shark Tank"-style pitch for "venture capital." The steering committee reviews the progress of funded projects monthly, ensuring that they are executed on time and on budget, and that they're delivering the expected value.

Finally, when it comes to accelerating a transformation program, practitioners must be adept at *(8) Agile ways of working.* Agile plays a core role in how transformation programs in general—and transformation networks in particular—run. Tony Thomas, CIO of $106 billion Japanese automaker Nissan Motor Corporation, stated bluntly in our interview, "The hierarchy, the rigidity, you have to let go of all that. You have to be a nimble, agile team that can drive outcomes very quickly."

Usually, promoting agility is no one's job or focus. It's expected to occur naturally, but (surprise!) it doesn't.

Here, "Agile" refers to the practices associated with the *Agile Manifesto,* published in 2001, which describes an approach to software development that prioritizes customer feedback, iterative design, and constant progress (among other things).[6]

This manifesto spawned a bevy of related frameworks. In fact, the world of Agile suffers from buzzword bingo and acronym overload—Lean, Scrum, SAFe, LESS, XP, Crystal, Kanban. Unfortunately, thanks to the hype and jargon surrounding Agile methodologies, many senior business leaders are leery about applying them. There's a vague sense that Agile methodologies can optimize things like software development, but when it comes to orchestrating a wider transformation, their utility is often unclear.

Agile ways of working can be extremely valuable when it's time to orchestrate a digital business transformation. As Tricia Blair, CDO of

Aon plc, noted, "Digital transformation is also about becoming more agile, not just in terms of following an Agile delivery methodology, but actually becoming more agile in the way we think, that infusion of 'test and learn.'"

Nearly all the sophisticated digital business transformation programs that we've seen incorporate Agile ways of working. Therefore, let's briefly examine the role that Agile can play in a transformation. (To be clear, we are not suggesting that the entire company needs to adopt Agile. Instead, confine Agile to the work of executing the transformation.)

$20 billion Netherlands-headquartered financial services provider ING Group provides a strong argument for Agile ways of working. The company knew it needed to rethink its business in the face of changing customer expectations and intense competitive pressure from fintechs. In 2014, ING Group released its guiding objectives in the form of its *Think Forward* strategy. One key goal was to digitally enable all the company's customer touch points. The executive team recognized that customer expectations had risen, thanks to their experiences with companies like Google, Facebook, and Uber.

A second goal was to digitize the company's processes end-to-end, enabling it to cut costs and increase the speed at which it could operate. In an update to its strategy in 2016, CEO Ralph Hamers committed to investing about $900 million for digital transformation, with the goal of achieving about $1 billion in annual cost savings by 2021.[7]

To accomplish these goals, ING first began using Agile in its corporate IT department in 2012.[8] It then extended Agile to transform the way its employees developed new customer offerings. In 2015, the company initiated a wholesale change in its headquarters staff, reducing the number of job types from 85 to 15 and eliminating the role of traditional full-time manager. This change, accomplished within two months, affected 3,000 people.[9]

Employees were asked to reapply for positions structured according to an Agile approach. ING divided the workforce into 350 "squads," each with a maximum of nine employees. Each squad owned a specific customer-focused business objective, and included workers from multiple disciplines, such as IT development, product management, marketing, and distribution. The squads functioned as "self-organizing" units, each setting its own direction, tasks, prioritization, and strategy for accomplishing its goals. The squads were coordinated using a formal approach, including "chapters" to connect members of the same discipline across different squads, and "tribes," which were groups of squads working on related missions. Agile coaches were embedded in the squads and tribes to facilitate the process and drive the cultural change needed to succeed in this new way of working.[10]

"We can't do transformation in the regular way, not just moving from waterfall to Agile, but we actually need to be completely encompassing, and we need to understand how the business is running, what our challenges are, and how we bring all of this together," said ING's COO and Chief Transformation Officer Roel Louwhoff. "So, we built what we call an 'Obeya' room."

Automotive manufacturer Toyota pioneered the use of Obeyas, which can be translated as "war room" in Japanese. "This is the heart of ING's transformation," Louwhoff said. "The purpose is simple: having the full overview of the status of all projects and solving issues quickly. If an issue can't be solved in five minutes, it's escalated to the next level. You immediately see how everything fits together."[11]

Similarly, at Australia's Bankwest, "we wanted to reconstitute our business around a number of tribes or multidisciplinary teams that are oriented around specific customer outcomes, effectively dissolving all of the traditional hierarchies and silos that exist in most organizations," said CIO Andy Weir. This is the crux of how Agile relates to orchestration.

Agile ways of working also allow companies to shift from sclerotic development and "program management" approaches to a model of "continuous delivery" in which innovations are released much more frequently (in days or weeks, rather than months or quarters). As Cisco CIO Guillermo Diaz observed:

> At Cisco, we continue to shift toward dynamic teams that come together for the duration of achieving their goal, often for just a few weeks or months. Dynamic teams make it much easier to innovate because we don't have the hassle of constantly changing the org chart. Once together, our teams utilize a continuous devel-

opment model and toolchain. They also collaborate very closely, often across time zones. To connect team members from different locations and organizations, we use technologies like Cisco WebEx Teams to see each other via video, chat, and share documents. It's not enough to say, "Let's have an Agile mindset." We give those words teeth by providing the right education, collaboration tools, and culture.

When Luis Uguina, CDO of banking and financial services provider Macquarie Group Limited, first arrived at the company, "the normal time frame to move into production was four months. We wanted to be a digital company, so we needed to be able to move into production every week, which we now do. The big difference is that we can now identify any problems on a weekly basis, not every few months. So that's the secret."

Sprints are another basic aspect of Agile ways of working. Work takes the form of time-boxed iterations with well-defined outputs and standard checkpoints that allow for learning and changes. As Nick Coussoule, senior vice president and CIO at $12.9 billion health benefit plan Blue Cross Blue Shield of Tennessee, remarked, "As with all transformational initiatives, think big and act small. It can be exciting to envision the end game but realize it takes incremental steps with adjustments along the way."

As Randstad North America's Alan Stukalsky put it, experimentation and learning, as elements of Agile ways of working, have to be ingrained in execution and company culture, all the way up to executive leadership: "Try things out, learn from it, pivot, try something else out, learn from it, scale it out .... Not every part of a digital transformation should be expected to be a home run or a big hit. And be OK with that. That's something that may require leadership education, that they've got to be ready for. It's something that has to be within the culture of the company."

At Toyota Motor North America, Agile ways of working are moving from IT development to the broader ways in which the organization executes change. CDO Zack Hicks noted that:

In some cases, we've been delivering products in six days so that we have a minimal viable product after the first request. It's allowed us to operate at a much faster pace .... Now, two years later, we're actually influencing how vehicles are being designed. As we're designing the interior of the vehicle, we're pushing the rest of larger Toyota to move toward Agile. I've even built an Agile practice where I'm training the rest of Toyota in how to do Agile the Toyota way.

THE CAPACITY TO CHANGE

We devoted the second half of *Digital Vortex* to an organizational capability we called **"digital business agility."** We defined it simply as "the capacity to change," and explained how it allowed organizations to adapt constantly to the ongoing market changes created by the Digital Vortex.

Digital business agility consists of three core attributes—hyperawareness, informed decision-making, and fast execution—that work together to make organizations agile (see Figure 32).[i]

Fig. 32: Digital Business Agility

Source: Global Center for Digital Business Transformation, 2015-2019

Hyperawareness is about sensing changes in the company's environment, workforce, and customer base. It involves gathering relevant

---

i   For more detail on digital business agility, please refer to chapters 5-8 of *Digital Vortex*.

information wherever it exists in the value chain. This can be competitive data, customer data, supplier data, data about physical assets, and so forth.

Informed Decision-making is about using the information captured through hyperawareness to make the best possible decisions. This requires companies to be highly inclusive, tapping into collective knowledge and expertise, and seeking out the information, perspectives, and judgment needed to make optimal decisions. Informed decision-making must also be augmented with data analytics.

Fast Execution is the third element of digital business agility. It means executing the decisions in a timely and effective way. This involves dynamically allocating the right resources to where they're needed. Business processes need to be dynamic, too. To execute fast, companies need to rapidly generate new processes, deploy them, test them, change them, and learn from them as opportunities arise—before disruptive competitors exploit those opportunities first. Our research and experience working with hundreds of companies around the world consistently reinforce our belief that digital business agility is the basis of "how to compete" with disruptors, all of which display high levels of agility. Agility is, therefore, something that is truly foundational to a company's success in the Digital Vortex. This capacity to change allows orchestrators to activate resources as needed, pulling them into the transformation, often temporarily, to address a particular demand.

The ability to draw on "burstable" expertise from an ecosystem of *people* resources, which we referred to in *Digital Vortex* as a "talent cloud," provides immense help to the functioning of transformation networks.

Data, as an organizational resource, is also important. For Zack Hicks, CDO at Toyota Motor North America, "A lot of digital transformation is unleashing the power of data and taking it out of the grips of each silo owner, and liberating the data and the insights so that the company can make better and faster decisions." *Infrastructure,* particularly IT assets, need to be dynamically orchestrated, and shifted quickly and seamlessly, when priorities change.

Digital business agility underpins connectedness, making the company what we called in our earlier book a "transformation-ready enterprise." Digital business agility creates the weak connections that provide new or relevant information and the strong connections that promote trust and cohesion in the organization.

Weak connections make us hyperaware because we can tap into ideas and data from a huge ecosystem of sources. They help us make informed decisions because we can access expertise and insights at the point of business need. They help us execute fast because distributed resources can be activated and shifted when and where needed.

Strong connections create hyperawareness, informed decision-making, and fast execution because information is transmitted more effectively, traversing the organizational, technological, and interpersonal barriers that trip up the execution of transformation programs.

CHAPTER 6
Organizing for Orchestration

WHO'S IN CHARGE AROUND HERE?

At most companies, digital business transformation—which requires major change across highly entangled functions—is a formidable test of the leadership team's ability to execute. Rarely do large incumbents have an organizational model that lets them effectively orchestrate this level of change. Most firms don't have anything remotely resembling an orchestration-oriented approach. For them, mobilizing resources and enabling their connections is a foreign concept altogether.

In this light, an argument rages among executives about whether digital should be a distinct entity unto itself or diffused throughout the business. In other words, should digital be "somebody's job" or "everybody's job"?

We've seen this debate break out in many workshops, including those with leaders from the same company! Our research reveals a sharp polarization of opinion on the issue, as shown in Figure 33.

Fig. 33: **Companies Are Divided on How "Digital" Should Be Managed**

Survey Q. Which of the following best describes how digital initiatives are perceived in your organization?

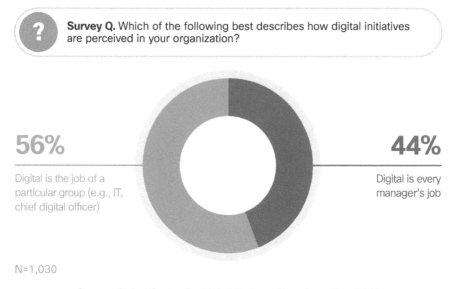

56%

Digital is the job of a
particular group (e.g., IT,
chief digital officer)

44%

Digital is every
manager's job

N=1,030

Source: Global Center for Digital Business Transformation, 2019

Although organizations are fairly evenly divided about whether "digital" should be a centralized or a distributed responsibility, our research shows that when it comes to managing digital *transformation,* 84 percent of organizations have established a dedicated or specialized group (see Figure 34). Here, we can see that digital (what for many people means digital *technologies)* should be viewed differently from transformation. For almost half of companies, digital is integral to every manager's job. However, this is not true for transformation, where more than eight in 10 companies recognize that transformation can't be added to managers' day-to-day activities, but instead must be aggressively driven in a targeted way.

Leaders would do well to bear in mind this important distinction, which we've stressed throughout: digital and transformation are not the same thing.

Fig. 34: Overwhelmingly, Companies Have Built a Dedicated Team Responsible for Driving Transformation

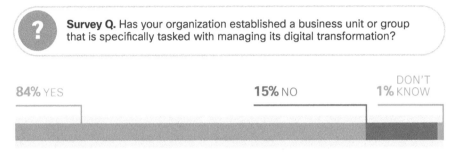

Survey Q. Has your organization established a business unit or group that is specifically tasked with managing its digital transformation?

84% YES   **15%** NO   DON'T **1%** KNOW

N=1,030

Source: Global Center for Digital Business Transformation, 2019

Although a critical mass of companies creates specialized units for transformation, we nonetheless find significant variation in how they manage transformation. Some companies do so at the functional, geographic, or business unit level. Others use centralized or cross-functional approaches. We've also seen a lot of trial and error as companies seek the right path. Figure 35 shows the divergent approaches to transformation governance that our research uncovered.

Fig. 35: Many Different Approaches to Transformation Governance

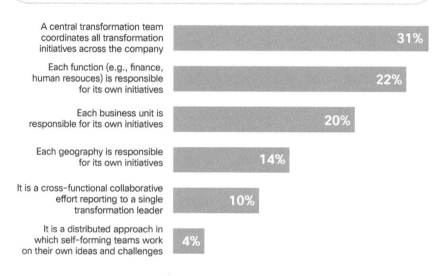

Survey Q. How are transformation initiatives primarily managed (e.g., coordinated, tracked) in your organization?

A central transformation team coordinates all transformation initiatives across the company	**31%**
Each function (e.g., finance, human resouces) is responsible for its own initiatives	**22%**
Each business unit is responsible for its own initiatives	**20%**
Each geography is responsible for its own initiatives	**14%**
It is a cross-functional collaborative effort reporting to a single transformation leader	**10%**
It is a distributed approach in which self-forming teams work on their own ideas and challenges	**4%**

N=1,030

Source: Global Center for Digital Business Transformation, 2019

The centralized versus diffused debate has gone on for a long time in a slightly different context: innovation. One school of thought holds that you need a Bell Labs, a Xerox PARC, or an X (formerly Google X, a subsidiary of Google's parent company, Alphabet) that sits apart from the mainstream of the business. Here, minds and creative energies can run free, unshackled from the stifling constraints of the corporate mother ship. Another school of thought maintains that this innovation paradigm is archaic. The best innovations come from all kinds of unexpected places, the nooks and crannies of the business, and even from outside the company proper (i.e., open innovation).

Centralization and diffusion both have downsides. With centralization, there can be throughput limitations. The centralized group may not have enough resources to keep pace with the extent and speed of change, or to drive it effectively. A centralized model can impede execution if a large number of decisions have to be considered, taken, and communicated by a small few. In addition, a centralized model can foster resentment and resistance if the business perceives the central group as an enclave of aloof outsiders: the kings and queens of PowerPoint.

A centralized transformation group can quickly become its own silo. As Norm Fjeldheim, CIO at $3 billion US genomics leader Illumina, explained in our interview:

> We don't run a centralized PMO because that becomes a choke point. We created a virtual PMO and decentralized the PMO resources into each of my functional teams so that they can all run parallel projects on separate project tracks and reduce friction.... That's how we went from essentially one big project to over 120 projects in one year.

By the same token, a diffused model can also slow down execution. Things can get lost in translation. Wheels can get reinvented. Coordination costs can increase. DooWhan Choi, CDO of $54 billion Korean steel producer Posco Group and CEO of POSCO ICT, told us that, "instead of covering just certain areas, we wanted to promote change systematically and consistently. To do that, we needed a dedicated organization. It simultaneously promotes new technology education, infrastructure, and data standardization."

ENTER THE COORDINATI

Amid all this, a lot of organizational resources end up getting thrown at the issue of transformation. As we demonstrated in the introduction, executives amply recognize the urgency to change in the Digital Vortex. This urgency creates a flurry of activity, one manifestation of which is a proliferation of overhead roles that are stirred into the organization to manage change. We've dubbed these resources the *coordinati*. They're the people whose job it is to make sure "stuff aligns."

In many large and midsized organizations, coordinati grow like mushrooms as teams (separately) invest in program management roles that get tied up ensuring that other groups have visibility into their work, and that they, in turn, understand how the work of other groups pertains to their own. Former Google CEO Eric Schmidt referred to these workers as "glue people"—employees "who sit between functions and help either side but don't themselves add a lot of value."[1] Glue is helpful in binding things together, but unhelpful when it makes things immovable.

Despite the fond wishes of those who hire them, coordinati almost always do the opposite of what they are assigned to do: they *slow down* change. They slow it down because they introduce more complexity. The coordinati create levels of debate (called "socialization" in their language) that throw sand into the gears of execution by slowing decision cycles, calling out exceptions and the need for customization, or otherwise privileging complexity. Their competing frameworks and tools exacerbate organizational entanglement instead of alleviating it.

In some cases, this occurs because the coordinati have no turf other than a small organizational toll booth from which they act as gatekeepers on the speed and extent of change. Hence, organizational change, and their role in it, becomes the turf that they protect. If everything is simplified and moving fast, why are coordinati required? No one likes to be so good at their job that they put themselves out of work. In short, the coordinati tend to bureaucratize transformation programs and aggravate execution complexity by increasing the density of discussion and decision-making.

Coordinati are a phenomenon born of organizational silos and a jumbled approach to change, where leaders act like 5-year-olds playing football, all chasing the ball at once, rather than playing their respective positions. Coordinati tend to make point-to-point bilateral connections, interfacing between two functions, for example, rather than multilaterally interlocking across the business to drive change in the way that "instruments" or transformation networks do.

Some digital czars, often brought into companies with great fanfare as "change agents," end up assuming the role of *coordinato de tutti coordinati* (the coordinator of all coordinators). They become marginalized bosses of change portfolios that the business has tuned out, left to lead a dead letter office.

Disempowered low- or midlevel bureaucrats who do "strategy and planning" for a given team are appropriate in the Change Management Zone. But in the Orchestration Zone, these roles gum up the works. Orchestrating cross-functional resources in the form of agile, execution-oriented transformation networks is utterly different from the misguided busywork of the coordinati and their bosses.

But coordinati are a symptom, not a cause, of the inertia that often bogs down change programs. The underlying driver of inertia is a lack of clarity about *who is responsible* for transformation, a mandate that is often scrambled into many roles and remits across the company. Thus, it should come as no surprise that our survey of global executives revealed a cross-section of C-level executives who are involved in their company's digital transformation.

The executives responsible for transformation run the gamut, as shown in Figure 36. Moreover, for 54 percent of our survey respondents, it's not one boss's job. Instead, multiple executives (in fact, an average of 3.3 different leaders) are "responsible for overseeing digital transformation" in the company, even though a dedicated transformation group exists.

Fig. 36: A Wide Range of Transformation Bosses

Survey Q. Which, if any, executives in your organization are responsible for overseeing digital transformation?

39%	38%	38%	29%	25%
Chief Executive Officer	Chief Information Officer	Chief Digital Officer	Chief Operating Officer	Chief Strategy Officer

22%	18%	15%	1%	1%
Chief Data Officer	Chief Marketing Officer	Chief Customer Success/Customer Experience Officer	Other	None

N=1,030

Source: Global Center for Digital Business Transformation, 2019

FAQ: CDO?

The chief digital officer role has emerged as one of several key leadership roles in digital business transformation. Some companies feel passionately about the need for a CDO. Others say, "You'll never see a CDO at Google. That would be like having a chief radio officer at the BBC. They're digital natives, and don't have a need for it." They predict that this trend will solidify in other companies over time.[2]

Charlotte Lindsey-Curtet, who leads digital transformation at the International Committee of the Red Cross, said, "CDOs are a bit like the Green Party. They're not yet completely mainstream, but they now have a seat at the table. And there's a general sense that they have an important point of view that should be understood." Our dealings with C-level leaders worldwide confirm that the CDO role is often ambiguous, fraught, and varies substantially across organizations.

Thus, one of the most common questions in our workshops is, "Should we hire a CDO?" And then: "If so, what should this person do?" For some, these questions are proxies for questions about how to organize for transformation, especially because the terms "digital" and "transformation" are so frequently conflated. So let's spend a few moments on the issue of CDOs.

In recent years, many Global 1000 companies and public-sector entities have created CDO roles. As noted earlier, the DBT Center's latest research found that 65 percent of large and midsized organizations have appointed a CDO.

This research has uncovered three main types of CDOs:

1. **The Customer Experience Maven.** The first type of CDO is focused predominantly in the areas of marketing, communications, e-commerce, customer engagement, and product development. Many of these CDOs come from a chief marketing officer role or from the advertising and creative industries. This CDO frequently views digital primarily as a way to position and strengthen the company's brand and to interact with customers. A key focus may be adding digital capabilities to existing products (e.g., placing a sensor on a refrigerator, putting a computer screen in a car). Roughly 25 percent of CDOs fall into this category.

2. **The Artist Formerly Known as the CIO.** The second type of CDO drives digital primarily from an IT perspective, much as the chief information officer has done in years past. Often, there is little change in the charter of the role, meaning the executive has oversight of the company's IT but gets a new business card. Sometimes, this is very superficial. The "D" is viewed as trendier than the "I," which, fairly or unfairly, carries certain baggage in terms of perceived value and skills. Indeed, CIOs as a profession have experienced a "crisis of relevance" in recent years, as business executives consistently cite lack of strategic alignment and innovation as challenges they see in IT leadership.[3] In some circles, there is a belief that if the company hires a CDO, it's because the CIO has not done his or her job. As many as two-thirds of CDOs are basically CIOs with a title change or a modest enlargement of their responsibilities.

> The chief transformation officer is responsible for mobilizing organizational resources and enabling their connections. He or she should act as the company's synergy creator.

3. **The Agitator.** The third type of CDO is hired not just as a "digital" leader, but to be a gadfly—to challenge received wisdoms and entrenched approaches—and in some cases, as one executive put it, to "blow up the business model" of the company. Many of these CDOs come from startup or management consulting backgrounds. Here, the focus is on major changes to firm strategy and helping the company make money in new ways, usually in response to disruptive competition and/or changing customer demands. This often happens when executive leadership wants to pursue offensive strategies like Disrupt or Occupy. About 10 percent of CDOs are "Agitators."

During its relatively short existence, the CDO role has been marked by tumult. Our research has found that the average tenure of a CDO, meaning the time between hiring and departure, is a little over two years. As companies experiment with this role, some are finding that ill-defined charters, turf wars, and other factors are leading to slow or failed progress. This causes them to question whether creating a CDO position was a wise choice. Some industry watchers are already forecasting the demise of the CDO as a leadership role, particularly as CIO and COO positions evolve.[4]

To the pervasive question of whether to hire a CDO and what his or her role should be, our response is, "Which type of CDO are you talking about?" "CDO" is merely an acronym. So instead of devoting energy to the questions above, we recommend that companies focus on a different query: "What is the best way to empower the business with digital capabilities?"

In terms of who should lead, we side with Baron Concors, former head of digital transformation at Pizza Hut, a division of Yum! Brands. He said that if you ask employees who's responsible for transformation, and you get a lot of different names, "then you really have to ask yourself who's in charge," and that "having one person who's accountable for driving the results and the organizational alignment around that is very important."[5]

THE NEW CTO: CHIEF TRANSFORMATION OFFICER

Who is the mysterious "orchestrator" to whom we have alluded throughout this book? Who is it that conducts the Transformation Orchestra?

The person tasked with running digital business transformation can be a senior leader with a variety of titles. And yes, this can include CDO. CDOs, despite the unsettled and variable nature of their role in the C-suite, are a logical vantage point from which to lead transformation. In fact, the majority of practitioners we interviewed for this book are CDOs.

However, because we've taken such pains to underscore that "digital" and "transformation" should not be confused, we humbly suggest a different title that's more in keeping with the nature of orchestration: ***chief transformation officer (CTO).*** Importantly, this should not be confused with another "CTO," the chief technology officer. The CTO, or whatever you choose to call this position, is the senior-most transformation practitioner in the company.

(If you want to create an orchestration practice within your company, feel free to give the person leading that work whatever title makes sense for your organization; we'll just use CTO for now.)

More and more, we are actually seeing companies use the "chief transformation officer" title.[6] Several interviewees for this project, including ING's Roel Louwhoff and Intuit's Al Ko, hold that title.

This position should be invested with an orchestration charter and responsibility for how the transformation program is executed. The CTO should be responsible for mobilizing organizational resources and enabling their connections. He or she should act as the company's *synergy creator*. In the words of one practitioner, "Every action I take can't just knock over the next domino. It has to knock over 10 or 12 dominoes."

Ideally, the CTO will report to the CEO. However, in some companies, this may not be practical or desirable. In these cases, reporting to the CIO or COO may be the best option. Whatever the arrangement, the position must be senior enough to command the respect of leaders company-wide. Making the CTO a direct report of the CEO is the simplest way to do this.

Matt Anderson, CDO and president of Arrow Electronics, echoed this in our interview when he stressed the need for a transformation "champion" with support from the highest levels of the business: "I think that they need to have a CEO-level reporting relationship because it's going to take

Transformation leads are usually senior, high-potential leaders with actual business responsibility. They're not coordinati. They can help with two-way communication into and out of the business, serving as evangelists for the transformation, and aiding the CTO in mobilizing the right resources from their particular functional area for inclusion in a transformation network.

that in order to break through inertia, roadblocks, territorialism, those kinds of things inside of a company."

The CTO should lead the company's *transformation office.* The work of the transformation office will be both surgical (episodic mobilization of specific transformation networks) and foundational (ongoing enablement of all resources through digital business agility). It will invest in efforts that target a highly specific business imperative (e.g., the successful launch of BikeCo's platform) and those that increase the connectedness of the organization in general.

There is no "rule of thumb" for how big a transformation office should be, but for a medium-sized incumbent, it might comprise about 50 people. For a very large multi-national company, it might be 200 people. (These are only ballpark estimates; your transformation office should be tailored to suit your company's unique needs.)

The transformation office should be lean and mean, not a sprawling overlay organization. You want to keep the team small because it will be an operating expense. Don't be tempted to convert the transformation office to a P&L; it's there to drive change and to stand up and incubate new capabilities, not to manage maturing businesses over time.

Although transformation networks will rely on a wide range of resources, they shouldn't all be centralized in the transformation office (that's the whole point of orchestration!). The transformation office must draw on resources from *throughout* the company, including IT.

ORGANIZATIONAL FABRIC

We said earlier that Org Structure is a vital instrument in the Transformation Orchestra, but it's most valuable when combined with other instruments. In music, rarely would anyone want to hear crashing cymbals all by themselves. While cymbals are great for punctuating a piece of music, adding to its power, there's a reason Bach never composed any concertos for cymbals.

When CEO Ulrich Spiesshofer established ABB's CDO role, he decided not to build a whole new organization separate from the rest of the business. Instead, he created a small but powerful team to enable digital transformation across the company.

Guido Jouret described ABB's approach this way:

> I'm reporting to the CEO. We've defined the role of the chief digital officer in the organization *not* to create a "Digital ABB" as a separate entity, to go out and raise the pirate flag and create something completely different. By contrast, we want to be as closely integrated with the core business as possible. The analogy I would use is that our mission and purpose are to make the rest of ABB more digital. I use terms like catalyst, transformation agent, enabler and provider of shared resources that can make other teams go faster.

Jouret's role in ABB was less *implementer* of the transformation and more *enabler.* Implementation was left to the operating units that understood the particulars of the business much better than he did. Left unchecked, though, the operating units would likely have built their own solutions—solutions incompatible with the rest of the organization and the wider transformation ambition. The solutions would have been locally optimized, probably at the expense of global efficiency or effectiveness. For example, a digital automation solution for the marine division might be built independently from a digital automation solution for the power grid division, despite significant technical and business process overlap.

We recommend that you introduce orchestration as a mode of execution that sits astride the *existing* org structure. Imagine enveloping the current org chart with a virtual **organizational fabric,** weak and strong connections, supported by digital business agility, which makes a connected approach to change possible. Technology networks, such as the internet or a corporate wide area network (WAN), are sometimes described as fabrics. That's because when you represent the nodes and connections of a network visually, their dense, overlapping, interconnected nature resembles a piece of woven cloth.

Our choice of fabric as an organizational construct was driven, in part, by several interviewees, who used a related word to describe a connected approach to transformation. That word was "thread." As a verb, it means "to interweave between." So, for example, a transformation office is a thread *interwoven* in the organizational fabric of the business.

A common way to "thread" the organizational model is by appointing *transformation leads* from individual teams and business units. These people sit in the business, but have a dotted-line reporting relationship with the CTO. They act as liaisons between their "home" in the business and the transformation office. They help thread organizational resources of people, data, and infrastructure from their part of the business.

Transformation leads are usually senior, high-potential leaders with actual business responsibility. They're not coordinati. They've been assigned as interfaces to the transformation office, but it's not their day job. They are expert in the day-to-day running of their area of responsibility, and can represent the on-the-ground reality that the transformation office needs to know. They also serve as the transformation office's internal clients.

Transformation leads can help with two-way communication into and out of the business. They serve as evangelists for the transformation, and aid the CTO in mobilizing the right resources from their particular functional area for inclusion in a transformation network. By stitching all the relevant resources together to execute as one, companies can take a more holistic view of the capability gaps and how they should be addressed across the entire value chain.

Transformation leads can also mitigate what one practitioner called the "catapult problem." This occurs when "new systems, policies, and other forms of enablement from 'corporate' are loaded onto catapults and fired, sending their contents to different groups and regions, their payloads exploding on impact. There's precious little thought given to how those on the receiving end can actually make use of those tools or what their effect will be."

Designating transformation leads is an approach used by many of the companies we researched, including Cisco, KFC, Sprint, and TechnipFMC. For example, at $11 billion French corporate and investment banking firm Natixis, Chief Digital and Technology Officer Luc Barnaud told us, "We have set up a community of ambassadors. We have about 50 ambassadors, so one per business domain, as well as one per specific function domain, like Compliance, Risk, and so on." Barnaud said the company convenes this team regularly to "share practices and projects across the community. And also to present them new initiatives they could launch, and how we can support [them] at a centralized level through my team."

At ABB, CDO Guido Jouret directly controls a team of about 200 people, but he indirectly controls hundreds more, thanks to the use of transformation leads. (ABB calls them "digital leads.") These leads are respected, high-level employees who operate within the business units and have an indirect reporting line to Jouret. They act as local digital evangelists, helping to push digital solutions and transformation agendas within each of the businesses. Jouret noted, "There's no way that I can respond to everything that's happening within my team, and in fact, we need to infiltrate, if you will, and in a positive way, these business units. I asked for every BU and every division to nominate a digital leader."

A "fabric"-style organizational construct, where a centralized group partners with the business through designated leads in a dotted-line reporting structure, is not necessarily revolutionary. Centers of excellence, matrixed (or "federated") structures, and hub-and-spoke models are common examples of how companies have tried to balance centralization and diffusion in designing their organizations. Many companies

The Must-HAVEs

What should you look for in a chief transformation officer? In collaboration with German leadership consultancy metaBeratung, the DBT Center surveyed more than 1,000 business executives across the world's largest economies on the skills they need to be effective transformation leaders.

We found that executives (and chief transformation officers in particular) must exhibit four key traits to be good digital business transformation leaders: they must be (1) **H**umble, (2) **A**daptable, (3) **V**isionary, and (4) **E**ngaged ("HAVE").

Humble

Adaptable

Visionary

Engaged

Source: Global Center for Digital Business Transformation, 2017-2019

Being **humble** involves accepting feedback and acknowledging that others know more than you.

(Continued on next page)

The Must-HAVEs

(Continued from previous page)

Humility means trusting an army of people who can help deliver the needed scale that one leader never could.

Being **adaptable** means accepting that change is constant and that changing your mind based on new information is a strength, not a weakness. An entrepreneurial and innovative mindset is one element of this adaptability.

Being **visionary** means having a clear sense of long-term direction, even in the face of short-term uncertainty, and an ability to see around corners, particularly in terms of how markets will evolve, what customers will value, and how digital technologies and business models will impact competition.

Being **engaged** is perhaps the most important trait of a successful transformation leader—particularly the ability to communicate the transformation's strategic and financial rationales to a constellation of different stakeholders.

have pursued "bimodal"[7] or "ambidextrous"[8] organizational models where they "exploit" mature businesses and "explore" disruptive innovations. However, these approaches have met with mixed results because they create bifurcation in how the company operates, introducing inefficiencies and still more silos.[9]

Even in matrixed organizations, fragmentation remains a big problem. The dual reporting chains, which are a hallmark of matrixed approaches, amount to a Band-Aid for dealing with organizational entanglement. They're way too limited to bridge silos and create meaningful synergy.

By contrast, the approach we describe here is not just about reporting lines or creating a second IT organization (though the transformation office may house certain technical skills and invest in, and build, digital solutions). When you work in the Orchestration Zone, what's truly different is that *separate does not mean disconnected.*

Orchestration provides the best of both worlds, where centralization and diffusion can coexist. A threaded, fabric-style organizational construct offers centralization (the transformation office) *and* diffusion (transformation networks and transformation leads within the business). This promotes *both* weak connections (access to new or relevant information from diffused resources) and strong ones (close ties among practitioners and business stakeholders that create trust and cohesion).

This is where digital makes all the difference versus the matrixed structures of the past. Digital technologies let organizations work together, and change, in a dramatically more connected way. In effect, they are becoming metaphorical "needles" that thread the connections between resources, helping to weave the organizational fabric.

For example, organizational network analysis applications use data from collaboration systems to generate detailed network maps of communication patterns between people, enabling companies to "see" how their employees do their jobs, how teams function, and who the "connectors" and "hidden influencers" are. This visibility is helpful for practitioners in understanding capability gaps, but also in defining "to-be" states in the execution of transformation networks.

Collaboration platforms continue to evolve at a rapid pace, empowering people to work together however they want, whenever they want, wherever they want, and to share information. This flexibility makes it easier for people involved in a transformation network to contribute to the effort and to interact in ways that create trust and cohesion within a virtual team.

> Assign all the change efforts that fall into the Orchestration Zone to the chief transformation officer to orchestrate in concert with the business.

Data has historically been locked in silos —trapped inside one group's data mart or data warehouse, or even on users' individual devices. Consequently, most organizations are hampered in changing because they don't make optimal use of the information they possess. Data virtualization technology is changing that, allowing workers to access information from different sources, regardless of its physical location or how it's formatted. With virtualization technology, a technical abstraction layer permits users to access information in real time no matter what it looks like, wherever it resides in the company, without the need for costly data replication or even systems integration. This "freeing" of data dramatically increases the number of weak connections in the company, allowing transformation networks (and everyone) to tap into valuable data when needed.

Similarly, cloud-based IoT asset management systems provide companies with real-time status of all manner of infrastructure, whether it's a mobile phone in an employee's purse or a pump on an oil platform in the North Sea. AI and automation are transforming inanimate infrastructure into intelligent agents capable of autonomously taking action when specific conditions are met. Infrastructure will increasingly interact with other infrastructure—without the need for human involvement, as in the case of so-called "lights out" factories, where no workers are involved (so there is no need for lighting). Thus we see the impact of digital technologies extends beyond understanding resources: they enable organizations to effect change—in other words, to get work done in new ways. These intelligent applications and systems afford practitioners new tools in coping with entanglement and making a connected approach to change a reality.

> The job of the network operator is not only to mobilize resources and enable their connections but also to manage the execution of a transformation network. He or she steers the work of its associated resources to produce a new process or a better capability.

Although a company should have a single leader responsible for executing the digital transformation, because of the networked nature of change in the Orchestration Zone, no CTO is an island. He or she, as the top transformation practitioner, must possess a new set of skills that hinges upon working effectively with many different types of resources across organizational boundaries (see sidebar "The Must-HAVEs").

All these skills play a role in helping to navigate the transformation dilemma of entanglement, but the ability to engage with both senior leaders and "worker bees" is paramount. CTOs must be highly engaged with the business, even as they stand up new capabilities outside the mainstream of the organization in the service of the guiding objectives and the overall transformation ambition.

The CTO will depend on support from, and collaboration with, other senior executives to drive change. Without the backing of other key leaders, these efforts will be too isolated, making the chances of transformation success vanishingly small.

As Sprint CDO Rob Roy noted in our interview, "Really, digital transformation is about the people and how you transform their mindset and get them involved. We've had much more acceleration as we've involved the larger company than we would in just the siloed department of [my] team."

LET LEADERS LEAD

As Thomas Gewecke, CDO and executive vice president, strategy and business development at the $14 billion American entertainment company Warner Bros. Entertainment Inc., emphasized in our interview, digital impacts everybody, everywhere, in everything they do within the organization:

> Whether you're making movies or TV shows, or writing the software that forms our games, or distributing our content to television networks or movie theaters, or Netflix or iTunes, or even to Walmart in the form of a DVD or Blu-ray disc, or if you are engaged in any part of the creative aspect between the capturing of the content, and the creation of the final product, you are working with digital tools, you're working in the digital medium …. Digital has become a mainstream, fully distributed part of nearly every functional area in our business, such that every manager should develop a meaningful operating competency in digital.

Every manager should understand digital and seek to apply it to his or her area of responsibility. But *transformation* should be driven by a single leader—the chief transformation officer.

One key lesson we've learned is: *let leaders lead.* Allow the people who've made your company successful to do what they do. Of course, if they're not performing or are actively trying to undermine the leadership consensus (constantly revisiting and challenging the transformation ambition, for example), they should be replaced. But leaders also have influence and expertise. The company needs their buy-in and engagement for major changes to work.

Most organizations and their leadership structures are geared to operate the business, not transform it. Most leadership teams are not there to be change agents, but to deliver results. These results tend to be framed in the here and now—meeting shareholder expectations or addressing the urgent demands of today's customer.

Don't expect everyone to be orchestrators of cross-functional outcomes. Make that someone's full-time job—someone who can transcend silos, unstick log jams, and focus outside the immensely difficult task facing all other leaders in the company: operating the mainstream business efficiently and effectively.

"Let leaders lead" means leave all the change in the Change Management Zone to your business leaders. Making decisions and implementing change is the quintessence of what it is to be a manager. But assign all the change efforts that fall into the Orchestration Zone to the chief transformation officer to *orchestrate in concert with the business.*

Letting leaders lead extends to the CIO and COO as well. Having them concentrate on "run the business" considerations (which, by the way, should not carry connotations of being non-strategic) is appropriate. And they should play a driving role in change programs like Plain Old Change, which are fairly limited calibrations inside a discrete function; Blanket Adjustments, such as the global rollout of a new cloud-based enterprise application; and Smart X, such as moving to a digital factory or Industry 4.0 model for production. Of course, IT and operations resources (i.e., the people, data, and infrastructure controlled by the CIO and COO) are key to many of the instruments in the Transformation Orchestra (see Appendix 2), and will, therefore, play a central role in all manner of transformation networks.

Business leaders should be discouraged from creating large numbers of overhead coordinati roles that slow down cycle times or duplicate efforts. Instead, they should leverage the transformation office for big cross-functional work. A "transformation lead" from the business units with a dotted-line reporting relationship with the CTO can help. This is important for creating efficient scale and execution where everyone can contribute and where the business understands what's happening in the transformation office.

An orchestrator is there to catalyze and accelerate change, not to be a new sovereign who dictates the direction of the company. The idea that a digital business transformation leader will preside over the organization and its entire portfolio of change is either a mirage or folly.

Although the transformation office will be a major contributor to establishing guiding objectives, decisions on business model and strategy should ultimately be made by the senior leader in charge of a given business line. Executive leadership owns the overall strategy portfolio and the decision on the competitive end state encapsulated in the transformation ambition. The chief transformation officer is there to frame the issues, furnish expert advice (pertaining to, for example, market disruption, customer behaviors, and how to "size the prize"), and provide the process and tools for a decision.

While responsibility for how transformation is executed rests with the CTO, there is *shared accountability* with executive leadership for the results. Bankwest CIO Andy Weir noted that while his role, by definition, means he has responsibility for technology and transformation, "Every single member of the executive also has an accountability for the successful delivery and operation of the model."

The CTO doesn't need to (and shouldn't) own all digital projects or be in competition with the business for resources or power. Business and IT leaders should view this person as an important ally, not as a rival or interloper. That said, some tension between the business and the transformation office is both normal and productive. As Sprint CDO Rob Roy pointed out, "If someone's not complaining about you, you're not being innovative enough."

One of our interviewees told us it all comes down to how you position things with stakeholders in the business: "I tell them, 'I'm not a policeman and I don't want your job. My only KPI is your success. I'm here to help you win.'"

EXECUTING WITH TRANSFORMATION NETWORKS

The CTO and transformation office personnel are the orchestrators: they mobilize resources and enable their connections. But how do the new processes and better capabilities generated by the transformation networks actually get built? Who is developing the application, provisioning the service, testing and delivering the output?

The organizational resources (people, data, and infrastructure) in a transformation network "do the work." The transformation office concentrates and directs business architecture mapping, communications, and the other orchestration competencies (see Figure 30) to help the transformation network execute its job of producing a new process or a better capability, a new way of doing something.

A large or midsized incumbent will likely have several transformation networks operating in parallel to address challenges that align with its various lines of business. The CTO is responsible at this "network of networks" level—that is, for the entire transformation program. However, he or she cannot realistically be expected to oversee several transformation networks in minute detail. That responsibility must rest with an individual who is a part of the transformation network—someone with visibility and control over its resources and connections. We call this role the *network operator.*

The job of the network operator is not only to mobilize resources and enable their connections but also to manage the execution of a transformation network. He or she steers the work of its associated resources to produce a new process or a better capability. As members of the transformation office, network operators should report to, and collaborate with, the CTO, sharing progress, prioritizing activities, and dismantling blockages.

Connectivity creates the conditions for connectedness.

A network operator serves as an "Agile head coach" for the transformation network he or she manages. Network operators use Agile ways of working to design, develop, and deploy new processes and better capabilities. This may involve a lot of applications for things like continuous development and integration (e.g., Jenkins, Atlassian's Jira); version control (e.g., Git, Apache Subversion); platform as a service (e.g., ServiceNow, Salesforce.com's Heroku); and "container" orchestration (e.g., Docker, Kubernetes).

Network operators must also collaborate with one another to synchronize the work across the transformation networks. Transformation networks shouldn't be execution silos. Figure 38 illustrates how this looks in a company like BikeCo, which has three transformation networks executing at once.

Transformation leads are key partners of the network operators. They can help mobilize resources from the various functions they represent, serving as a "brain trust" of advisers, as well as communicating the work of transformation networks back to the business.

Fig. 38: Managing Transformation Networks

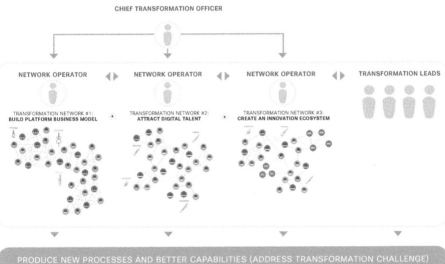

Source: Global Center for Digital Business Transformation, 2019

The new processes and better capabilities that are the outputs of transformation networks address the transformation challenge at hand, creating the "desired effect" of orchestration: improved business outcomes such as revenue or profit growth. But when it comes to *scaling* the new process or better capability, the output is transitioned to the core of the business. Very often, the resources that played a part in designing and building this output in the transformation office will then *use* that output on a daily basis.

For example, a key instrument in BikeCo's second transformation network, which addresses the need to attract digital talent, is Workforce Engagement. This instrument would very likely include subject-matter experts in talent acquisition: BikeCo's recruiters. These recruiters would contribute to, and help create, the new way of attracting digital talent. Once this output is ready for prime time, the network operator integrates the new process into the business, "relinquishing" its oversight and operation going forward. The recruiters become key users of the new process or better capability that they themselves helped shape. This approach attenuates the adoption challenges common to transformation programs because these resources are invested in the success of the effort.

Incubation takes place under the supervision of the network operator and the transformation office, but scaling and operation occur in the mainstream of the organization (transformation leads from the business can play a role in transitioning minimum viable products and other transformation outputs to the functions). This transition mirrors an Agile-related approach to digital technologies that is common in companies producing new processes and better capabilities at speed: DevOps.

With DevOps, there is an integrated "handshake" between the people who develop a solution and those who operate it. The transformation office remains connected to the outputs in order to make tweaks and iterations as feedback is received from users operating the new process at scale.

There are times for centralization and times for diffusion. As an *aide-memoire* for practitioners, we've created the following limerick:

> For creating the new, and when the time comes to incubate,
> The wise executive knows always to **separate;**
> But when the mood shifts to scale,
> Remember without fail,
> For operation and propagation, you **integrate.**

Transformation networks are the lynchpin in taking a connected approach to how change is executed. But why do transformation networks "work"? What is it about them that makes success more likely?

There are several factors. Transformation networks are great for clarifying the task of change. They have a specific job to do: close a capability gap presented by the organization's guiding objectives. This clarity provides guardrails for execution, de-cluttering what's in scope and what isn't.

Combining transformation networks in a network of networks helps the CTO create visibility for the organization in terms of what resources exist, how they interact (or don't), and their relevance to a given challenge. This visibility helps with the problem of "mutual adjustment," meaning it allows the left hand to know what the right hand is doing, and vice versa. Visibility also supports organizational learning. Each time the company transforms should be easier and more efficient than the previous time. The transformation office should systematically extract, document, and share learnings and assets from across the organization's transformation networks.

The orchestration competencies we've described help transformation networks to function properly, bringing together resources and allowing them to cooperate and work effectively. Digital business agility and Agile ways of working go hand in hand: connectivity creates the conditions for connectedness, which is what organizations need to flip the script on a string of failed transformation bids. Through weak connections, transformation networks can reach distributed resources that can contribute to the work of change. Through strong connections, they can operate with trust and cohesion, elements that are conspicuously absent in most cross-functional undertakings. The weak and strong connections that come with transformation networks are key ingredients in producing the synergy that makes for successful transformations.

When firms operate in the Orchestration Zone, there is a lot of potential value in terms of competitive gains. But doing so also comes with risk. The agility associated with a connected approach to change de-risks transformation because it divides the effort into smaller, simpler, and executable pieces that create momentum and provide opportunities for course corrections when things aren't working. When practitioners connect these pieces, they can successfully deliver digital business transformation—holistically and at scale.

CONCLUSION
Orchestration in Action

APPLYING THE CONCEPTS

This book is intended to spark a shift in mindset for transformation practitioners and how they conceive of change, and even a different way of looking at the organization itself. But in the book's opening, we did set the expectation that we would furnish the answer to the question "how?"—how do you execute a digital transformation program, one rooted in a connected approach to change?

At this stage, it's helpful to consider how to tangibly put into practice the different frameworks we've prescribed. Let's return to BikeCo to demonstrate how these concepts interconnect and allow companies to execute change in the Orchestration Zone.

Note that we won't introduce the various recommendations and frameworks in the same order in which we have presented them in this book. This is because they won't unfold in a simplistic, linear way in your company either. As with most things in the Digital Vortex, this is not a crude, serial process. Still, every journey begins with a single step; we all have to start somewhere. As a musical conductor or band leader might say, "Let's take it from the top!"

Appendix 4 provides our "Orchestrator's Cheat Sheet." It's a compendium of all the key actions for transformation practitioners that are explained in this chapter. This cheat sheet provides a handy reference summarizing 21 of our most critical recommendations for executing a digital business transformation.

Recognizing that BikeCo was facing new forms of competition and a softening in its core markets, the firm's CEO and board were ready to embrace digital business as a new way to grow revenue and boost margins. This embrace would mean playing defense in some areas of the business and going on offense in others.

With digital being a more prominent part of its future plans, the company knew a large-scale, complex transformation was needed. It was going to make major changes to its business that would affect employees across the board, in virtually all functions and divisions. Major change in a highly entangled environment like BikeCo meant the company would have to operate in the Orchestration Zone, mobilizing the organization's resources and enabling how they connected and worked together.

There might be some more standard organizational change going on in parallel, but the digital business transformation BikeCo's top management team envisioned, although its specifics had yet to be defined, was likely to be well beyond what they could accomplish with siloed change efforts led by individual managers in different corners of the company.

Action: When pursuing digital business transformation, embrace the need for a connected approach to change, and operate in the Orchestration Zone, rather than relying on ill-suited change management doctrines.

With this in mind, the company created a new position, that of chief transformation officer. The role was filled by Nisha Kumar, who came from outside the company, and in fact had no previous experience in the sporting goods business. She did have a retail background; she'd held a senior e-commerce role for a large specialty retailer and was an experienced transformation practitioner.

She was the kind of person who had a natural curiosity and was great at assembling teams. Her style was firm, but collaborative, not an authoritarian personality. The new CTO clearly relished a challenge and the opportunity to learn new things. She wasn't a techie, but had a deep understanding of digital business models, and had worked in strategy for a large management consultancy for more than a decade prior to moving into the retail world.

Finally, she was quick to win the respect of BikeCo senior and middle management through a series of introductory meetings, rapid-fire discovery, and stakeholder engagement. Within 90 days, even the most skeptical among BikeCo's old guard had to admit Nisha had acquired a strong command of the company's business lines, current-state operating environment, and market dynamics. In short, she brought to the table the "must-HAVE" leadership traits for the role: she was humble, adaptable, visionary, and engaged.

Action: Appoint a chief transformation officer. Hire someone who is humble, adaptable, visionary, and engaged.

As CTO, Nisha's charter was to drive BikeCo's digital business transformation. She had a clearly defined responsibility to oversee transformation in a holistic sense, but her boss, the CEO, knew her success depended upon other leaders in the business, so he established a shared accountability for the results. Nisha and the CEO spent a lot of time defining the role and its scope, which would focus on "disrupting" BikeCo in a positive way. The CEO wanted Nisha to help jolt the organization into doing new things, even if that meant taking some calculated business risks. She wouldn't own all the company's digital projects—at Bike-

Action: Make the chief transformation officer responsible for orchestrating the company's digital business transformation, mobilizing organizational resources and enabling connections among them, but create shared accountabilities and joint KPIs with the business for results. The rest of the business should focus on implementing digital capabilities and driving change in their respective areas.

Co, that was the preserve of the CIO and the business units—but rather would focus on cross-functional efforts that drove business model innovation and fostered growth. The rest of the business would worry about implementing digital capabilities in their respective areas.

Initially the plan had been for her group to be a part of the IT organization. Nisha constructively pushed back and stood her ground, insisting as a condition of accepting the role that she report directly to the CEO. Nisha knew that as part of the top management team, she would have the level of authority she needed to be successful. Executing the type of change expected of her would have been next to impossible if she were several rungs down the corporate hierarchy.

Action: Invest the CTO with a high level of seniority—not as a middle manager or one of the coordinati, but as a member of the executive team that holds sway in the organization.

In some of their initial conversations about the role, the CEO had suggested a bimodal approach, where Nisha would take over management of more than 100 IT personnel from the CIO and direct them in working on a variety of "next-gen" projects. Nisha was not an empire builder and had little interest in leading an organization like this. So, she demurred, explaining that a) she didn't believe digital business transformation was purely an IT exercise, and b) the last thing she wanted was for her arrival to create a "split personality" in how BikeCo operated. She didn't want the organization wasting precious time or capital on costly reorgs either.

Action: Build a transformation office under the CTO. Keep the team small and remember it should orchestrate most of the work associated with transformation, rather than performing it.

The CEO agreed and Nisha set about forming a small, nimble team of around 40 people, the BikeCo transformation office. She knew that she and the few dozen people who worked for her could not all by themselves deliver transformation at scale for the firm. She would have to orchestrate the resources from around the company, and from key partners and vendors who could provide both bandwidth and expertise she needed.

She carefully constructed the transformation office with a number of specific competencies she would need to pull off a complex orchestration of resources across the company. The first thing she did in building her team was to negotiate the transfer of a dozen business architects who had been a part of the company's large IT organization. These architects had a lot of institutional knowledge about the company's processes and systems; they immediately set to work mapping the organization's people, data, and infrastructure resources.

BikeCo was pretty average in terms of its digital capabilities. The firm wasn't using mimeographs, green-screen terminals, or fax machines to conduct business, but as the CIO himself conceded in his first meeting with Nisha, "This company still has a lot of growing up to do when it comes to digital solutions."

The IT department was pretty typical, too. Although it was moving toward Agile ways of working, this was really a long-term evolution. Like most IT shops, people in it spent the lion's share of their time "keeping the lights on."

One area in which Nisha perceived a clear across-the-board problem (not just in IT) was measurement. The company had little to no ability to measure digital initiatives and change efforts or the value they delivered. She brought in a talented financial modeler she had worked with in her consulting past to develop a consistent methodology for tracking work and quantifying shareholder value impacts.

Nisha's vision for the transformation office demanded an infusion of other new talent and some skills BikeCo didn't have in-house. She

Action: Engage resources that can model value impacts of transformation programs. This keeps efforts on track and creates support among stakeholders, especially senior management and the board.

didn't have the luxury of the long term, so she set up a meeting with BikeCo's chief people officer. Together, they devised a plan to hire a half-dozen Agile coaches. Nisha wanted a mix of hard-core technical skills and business savvy. Bike-Co's recruiters targeted early-in-career software developers and midcareer professional hires from consultancies.

Action: Prioritize hiring skill sets in the transformation office that reflect orchestration competencies like design thinking or business architecture. Look to an ecosystem approach to fill skills gaps, and be agile in your approach to engaging talent (i.e., develop a "talent cloud" for skills that are scarce, expensive, or just occasionally needed).

She also wanted to hire a few consultants from interactive agencies who had experience in customer journey mapping and design thinking. However, Bike-Co wasn't having any luck recruiting these people, especially in its small headquarters city in Massachusetts. She was certain that skills like these would help her stakeholders identify root causes, think creatively about solutions, and keep efforts centered on enhancing BikeCo's value delivered to customers.

These skills would be instrumental in creating the "jolt" to the organization the CEO had stressed from Day 1. She worked with ecosystem partners and staffing agencies to find these experts, engaging them as contract staff instead of hires.

Nisha made clear to the CEO and board she needed their steadfast support, not just when she was first hired, but consistently over time. She knew from her previous company that backsliding and opting out among managers sounded the death knell of transformation programs. To their credit, the CEO and board stepped up: in both executive leadership and company all-hands settings, the CEO reiterated time and again his unequivocal support for the transformation office and his expectation of all managers and employees that they "row toward the same lighthouse."

This was both a leadership behavior the CEO exemplified and a disciplined approach to organizational communications. In short, opting out was not an option. This didn't mean the company's plans were chiseled in stone—Nisha and her stakeholders would adapt them as they learned along the way and as conditions dictated—but there was a sense of constancy in how the executive team portrayed the change to the organization and in how they structured accountabilities.

Action: Ensure that the executive team consistently reinforces the direction of the transformation, along with their explicit expectation that managers and individual employees plan, invest, and execute in ways that support this direction.

The CEO and board also wanted Nisha to have the budget flexibility to do what was needed—to move with speed and agility. Accordingly, Nisha worked with the company's CFO to establish an internal venture fund, the $15 million BikeCo Transformation Fund, to grease the financial skids of execution and help accelerate projects.

Prior to her arrival, there was a vague awareness among the board and BikeCo's CEO of the need to change. There were also plenty of digital initiatives and pilots going on in various parts of the company, but they were piecemeal and were paying only modest dividends in terms of productivity gains and improved efficiencies associated with automation. Nisha and her team partnered with the CIO and quickly inventoried these projects to create a baseline understanding of where the company was digitizing; they updated it as new initiatives emerged. This was helpful in creating good governance processes and portfolio oversight.

Action: Create an appropriately sized internal venture fund that can accelerate cross-functional efforts and business outcomes.

When Nisha had been with the company for around five months, BikeCo closed the books on its fiscal year. The results were bad: revenue, margins, and market share all were down. The need to act on digital business transformation took on a palpable urgency.

Action: Document major digital initiatives occurring across the business to create visibility and potential synergies. The orchestrator, however, shouldn't try to "own" these projects.

Reeling from their disappointing results, Nisha and the executive leadership team traveled to a resort on Cape Cod for a pivotal planning meeting. One of the key resolutions from their offsite session was the formation of a working group to explore digital business opportunities that could jumpstart revenue growth and halt the slide in margins. Nisha, as CTO, was assigned to lead this team.

The working group comprised roughly 20 senior and midlevel executives who pored over data, met with outside analysts and partners, and considered the company's options. Nisha and key members of her team facilitated the group's work, serving as both project managers and "expert witnesses" on trends, market sizing, and customer data. The customer journey and design thinking gurus she had engaged helped the group work backward from the point of view of their customer: What do customers want? How are their behaviors and expectations evolving? How could we use digital to create value in new ways?

Action: Make the customer the centerpiece of your company's digital business transformation. Work backward from how you intend to create new or improved value for the end customer.

Looking across BikeCo's four major lines of business, the group determined that the company's components division presented some intriguing digital business opportunities, particularly with respect to its channel structure, which relied on a large network of independent bike stores and retail chains.

For the components business line, the working group recommended the pursuit of a platform model that could connect suppliers and BikeCo end customers in a new way. The head of the components business reviewed the plan and liked what she saw. The platform would create a lot of value for BikeCo's customers, including cost value (bicycle components would be cheaper), experience value (there would be more choice and convenience in how components were bought and sold), and especially platform value (there would be value from the new connections the platform represented). She endorsed a disruptive strategy and dubbed the new platform "BikeCo SHIFT." Platform value, a marketplace-oriented business model, and this disruptive strategy would serve as the "guiding objectives" of the transformation of this line of business.

Action: Set guiding objectives that include creating value for customers, delivering and capturing that value through an appropriate business model, and the strategy needed to make it happen. Guiding objectives must be set at the line-of-business level, not for the company as a whole. The leader of a given line of business, and ideally the entire executive team, must be supportive of these guiding objectives—it's not the job of the CTO to dictate these to the business.

For BikeCo's other lines of business, though, the working group saw less upside in an aggressive, disruption-oriented strategy. There, the identified opportunities were more "defensive," leveraging digital tools and technologies to streamline the business, ratchet down costs, and enhance the channel experience. The leaders from these lines of business pursued a strategy that called for them to "harvest."

With guiding objectives set across BikeCo's lines of business, Nisha worked with executive leadership to fortify things with a clear "transformation ambition." This statement encapsulated the full spectrum

Action: Pursue a portfolio of strategies, with different guiding objectives for each line of business.

of transformation efforts and the company's desired competitive state, where digital would become a significantly larger part of the equation in terms of sales. This was "50 in all 4 by 25," or 50 percent of revenues in all four lines of business coming from digital by 2025. This played a huge role in sustaining the disciplined communication the work demanded; it created awareness, understanding, and buy-in in terms of the company's direction. This had been sorely lacking in the company's workforce in years past.

The transformation office had its marching orders: build and incubate the BikeCo SHIFT platform for the bicycle components business, and

Action: Articulate a transformation ambition— the company's holistic change goal—that is precise, realistic, inclusive, succinct, and measurable (PRISM). Encourage senior leaders to become ambassadors of the change and stress the transformation ambition in their teams' communications and planning.

streamline operations and the channel experience in their other business lines. These challenges were cross-functional in nature and were compounded by the entangled nature of Bike-Co's organization. Nisha and her team turned to the Transformation Orchestra framework to consider the company's people, data, and infrastructure resources in a simple yet comprehensive way. Armed with the business architecture maps her team had compiled—a kind of drone-level view of the organization—they had a good handle on who did what and what various workflows and processes looked like. They knew what they had to work with—and what they didn't.

For the BikeCo SHIFT work, they determined the most important instruments for building this new model were Offerings, Channels, and Partner Engagement. These represented people, data, and infrastructure that were relevant to the three areas, but drawn from all over the company. For their more defensive challenges, they prioritized instruments like Culture, Incentives, Org Structure, and Workforce Engagement to get the right resources mobilized for the task at hand.

Operating in the Orchestration Zone meant that Nisha and her team would be mobilizing these resources and enabling the connections between them. They formed transformation networks to execute in building new processes and better capabilities. Each transformation network consisted of multiple instruments (and the resources they represented) that helped address the different challenges the company faced. They performed a capability assessment on the in-scope resources and found several deficiencies and gaps in talent, data availability and completeness, and connectivity to relevant assets. These helped the transformation office prioritize activities in executing the transformation.

Action: Create a business architecture map of the company spanning all the instruments of the Transformation Orchestra. Map the people, data, and infrastructure that exist, as well as their relationships and the workflows between them.

Action: Determine which instruments—and the organizational resources they represent—are most relevant to the transformation challenges presented by the company's guiding objectives.

BikeCo had three transformation networks operating concurrently: 1) building a platform business model (BikeCo SHIFT), 2) attracting digital talent, and 3) creating an innovation ecosystem. These were well-defined areas of execution with clear goals. This helped track progress and measure the value they delivered. Nisha was responsible for the success of all three of these transformation networks; this "network of networks" represented the company's full digital transformation roadmap, albeit in a nonlinear manner.

Action: Create transformation networks consisting of multiple instruments to address transformation challenges. Keep each transformation network small, agile, and focused on a highly specific transformation challenge. This makes measuring the progress and impacts of the change easier.

Each transformation network was led by a "network operator," one of the Agile coaches Nisha had hired. Each was responsible for mobilizing the resources needed for that transformation network, and for enabling the connections between them. They were also responsible for execution in building new processes and better capabilities. This included:

- Arranging customer journey mapping and design thinking workshops for the people involved

- Working with business architects to leverage the maps of organizational resources and their relationships

- Conducting capability assessments on those resources and prioritizing areas to target and improve

- Ensuring the people involved in the transformation network had the right collaboration tools and that relevant communications were flowing into and out of the transformation network

- Leveraging shared data repositories, development platforms, and "sandboxes" that would allow for rapid execution

- Getting software developers to write application programming interfaces (APIs) between disconnected data and infrastructure resources that were needed

- Using Agile ways of working to make progress in a series of iterative sprints

Unfortunately, Nisha discovered there were some bad actors on the BikeCo management team. Two executives were uncooperative and viewed the CTO role with barely concealed hostility. Nisha found, however, that the other seven members of the executive leadership understood the need for change, and although they had their normal run-ins, they were good-faith business partners of the transformation office.

Action: Encourage the CTO to build a strong rapport with division and functional leaders; rather than competing with the business, the transformation office should be seen as a source of innovation, agility, and speed.

As for the two executives who opposed Nisha's work, one was encouraged to spend more time with her family and ended up accepting an early retirement package. The other stewed in his juices. Because he didn't support the work of the transformation office, and was not effectively tapping into its funding or capabilities, he quickly found himself on the outside looking in. The performance of the division he oversaw dipped and key talent departed for greener pastures.

Nisha cultivated a close working relationship with several C-suite executives, including the CFO, CIO, and COO. Within a year, her team's work was a key feature on the critical path for all these executives and their groups. Nisha asked all key divisional and functional managers to appoint "transformation leads" from their teams to liaise with the transformation office on an ongoing basis. This brain trust of leaders would help Nisha steer the work of the

Action: Appoint "transformation leads" from other teams who can help thread execution across groups. Rather than creating a transformation unit that is a silo unto itself, weave an "organizational fabric" of connected execution on top of the existing org structure.

transformation networks that her group was spearheading. The transformation leads acted as two-way conduits for information—to and from the business units and functions they represented. Nisha found this engagement with stakeholders to be highly valuable in "threading" execution cross-functionally and in securing buy-in within the business.

Some of the resources involved in the transformation network tasked with building the BikeCo SHIFT platform were controlled by managers who had other priorities. The remaining bad actor on the BikeCo management team was particularly problematic. He kept saying he didn't have the budget for "that science project" and that his people were focused elsewhere.

Nisha made clear to him several things. First, the resources she was counting on to design and incubate the BikeCo SHIFT platform—those who came from this executive's organization—would be needed for a defined period of time to create the process changes and new capabilities that were its essence. When complete, after a series of key sprints, those human resources would be freed up again. Her team would handle creating the APIs to the relevant data sources and infrastructure assets he controlled.

Second, Nisha said she completely understood the budget challenges this executive faced. He wasn't accountable for delivering a platform—although it would be good for BikeCo overall, it wasn't really his problem. That's why she would be bankrolling the SHIFT platform entirely through the BikeCo Transformation Fund.

She also noted that in addition to the work going on to build BikeCo SHIFT, she was driving two other transformation networks: one on digital talent and the other on the company's innovation ecosystem. Both would benefit this executive in a concrete way, and neither had any real opportunity cost for him—they didn't demand resources from his organization, so were pure upside. She encouraged him to think about the transformation of the company more holistically, rather than getting stuck on the issue of how his resources were pulled into the creation of the BikeCo SHIFT platform.

When the executive still wasn't on side, and was undermining the work of the transformation office by directing the managers on his team not to work on the "distraction" the platform represented, Nisha had a sit-down with him. She explained that while she welcomed his input on the platform and what it would take to be successful, if he wanted to debate a) whether the BikeCo SHIFT platform would actually be built, or b) whether his resources would help in that, he could expect a call from the CEO. While she kept it as a last resort, Nisha knew she had a strong leadership consensus behind her and that she could invoke the CEO's mandate in the face of opposition.

When the work of the company's three transformation networks reached a threshold of maturity, ownership of their outputs transitioned from the transformation office to the mainstream of the business. In the case of BikeCo SHIFT, the divisional head of the components business appointed a new vice president to run the platform. Nisha's team remained involved and made tweaks and improvements as they received input from customers, suppliers, and salespeople.

Action: Keep the transformation office focused on incubating new processes and better capabilities. Transition ongoing management of these processes and capabilities when they reach maturity to the business. The transformation office should remain engaged to adjust the outputs over time.

Over the next several months, the new processes and better capabilities that were the fruits of the transformation networks Nisha's team had led were delivering: the BikeCo SHIFT platform beat its revenue targets. The other two transformation networks contributed bottom-line improvements and BikeCo's margins turned upward. The company was disrupting the disruptors and winning back market share.

As BikeCo's markets continued to evolve, Nisha and the transformation office turned to new transformation challenges that arose as the lines of business introduced still more business model pivots and strategies to ward off threats and capitalize on digital business opportunities. The transformation office had to be agile to launch, integrate, and retire transformation networks over time.

In addition to building and incubating new processes and better capabilities, and directing a connected execution approach through transformation networks, the transformation office had another, more foundational task. In addition to providing a jolt that would help shake things up at BikeCo, the CEO told Nisha he wanted her to improve the overall agility of the company: "Help us deliver faster on the new processes and better capabilities we need. But as a company, it feels like we're fighting with one arm tied behind our back. We're not in the vicinity of the 'digital natives' out there in terms of speed and agility."

Action: Ensure that the CTO works with other key leaders, particularly the CIO and the assigned transformation leads, to increase the overall level of digital business agility in the company—its foundational capacity to change. This involves creating weak connections among organizational resources that provide new or relevant information, as well as strong connections that create the trust and cohesion needed for a connected approach to change.

In this sense, Nisha's charter as CTO extended to enhancing the company's overall capacity to change. Her connected approach to organizational change was working, but she needed to create more connectedness in how the company operated as a whole—that was the key to sustaining change and making BikeCo a transformation-ready enterprise. Working with the CIO, COO, and the transformation leads assigned by the divisional and functional managers, Nisha pushed an agenda that would increase the hyper-awareness, informed decision-making, and fast execution capabilities of the organization. This required a comprehensive effort to gather information, use analytics and inclusive processes for decisions, and make processes and resources more dynamic so they could be used at the point of business need. Digital business agility became a kind of watchword among the transformation practitioners of the company.

In doing so, she created a lot of weak connections that allowed new or relevant information to move among organizational resources. She also fostered strong connections, particularly among BikeCo's people resources, to nurture the trust and cohesion they needed to work together effectively.

GETTING REAL

Perhaps you're thinking, "This may all be well and good for BikeCo. They're not even a real company for crying out loud!" But using the story of BikeCo to explain a connected approach to change is a necessity because there's no company we know of that's doing *all* these things. Our BikeCo illustration is just that—an illustration, a picture of how orchestration in a company can look from end to end. Moreover, BikeCo is actually an amalgam of several real-world organizations we've studied, organizations from both the private and public sectors that are making strides toward a more connected approach to organizational change.

If no one is doing all this today, why do we feel so strongly that a connected approach to change is right? Or that we need to conceive of organizational resources in a post-functional way (i.e., with "instrument" thinking)? Or that transformation networks can unlock a new way of executing organizational change?

First, we're not looking to spot and define the "trailing indicators" or chart one company's historical journey over a period of years as the exemplar of how to transform. No, we need the *leading* indicators, some of which may not be fully formed. Like Nisha at BikeCo, the clients we engage with don't have the luxury of the long term. As Nespresso's Cyril Lamblard remarked, "A year in digital is like a dog year."

Our task is not to prove an empirical relationship between a certain variable and a particular company performance outcome (recall the so-called Halo Effect). Rather, it's to scour a diverse and shifting landscape and make sense of, distill, and communicate what's working and, perhaps more important, what's not. As students of the Digital Vortex, we need to operate in a business milieu of turbulence and ambiguity. We therefore aspire to be far more agile in how we generate insights, unlike traditional academic research outputs with "best before" dates that precede their publication.

Second, as we explained in the introduction, this book is focused more on what nearly everyone gets wrong than on helping companies mimic high-profile stock market darlings or model their change efforts on greenfield startups and digital giants that are unrecognizable from today's "entangled incumbents." In terms of lessons learned, our research has revealed a ton of consistent mistakes, but also a large number of good practices and no-regret moves that companies can successfully use to fix their approach to change. These approaches have some discernible common threads, which we've detailed in these pages.

Virtually all the executives we've interviewed over the past two years portrayed their transformation efforts as works in progress, and displayed a healthy level of competitive paranoia. As KFC CDO Ryan Ostrom said, "If anybody says they're going fast enough on digital transformation, I want to know who they are. Because the one thing I've learned is that no one's moving fast enough." This was a major impetus for us in writing this book—everyone is in the same boat, doing their best, however imperfectly, to maneuver in the Digital Vortex.

Even among those companies we consider transformation leaders—those that have put a great deal of thought, innovation, and financial capital behind their approach—we have not detected even a whiff of triumphalism. In fact, everybody wants to know what everybody else is doing and is eager to learn. No one remotely thinks they have everything figured out.

And count us among that group. Although the DBT Center is uniquely positioned to listen to, learn from, and engage with large and midsized companies all over the world, it would be the height of hubris to say that we have all the answers when it comes to digital business transformation.

Driving change in the Orchestration Zone is no stroll in the park. For most large and midsized companies, digital business transformation can be a multiyear, globe-spanning endeavor. It will be rife with barriers and risk, and will demand some pretty next-level stuff of leaders. The journey will never be direct—you'll need to plot your path based on partial information, go down some blind alleys, and maybe even encounter some headwinds and intentional misdirection from obstinate colleagues along the way.

Still, most executives today know that, in the Digital Vortex, they don't have a choice. They must get transformation right. If not, their companies will find themselves on the sidelines—or in the graveyard.

BLOWN MINDS

Throughout *Orchestrating Transformation,* we've stressed the managerial challenges we all face in dealing with organizational change in an environment characterized by increasing scale, interdependence, and dynamism. The transformation programs we see in companies around the world look the way they do in large measure because our brains cannot effectively navigate the entangled state of our organizations.

When we confront the magnitude of change the Orchestration Zone represents, we bump up against not just the limits of mainstream management principles, but in fact the limits of the human mind and our cognition. As a species, we are not great at thinking in exponential, multidimensional, or networked terms.

The American economist and political scientist Herbert Simon, one of the forebears of today's field of behavioral economics, understood this and proposed the idea of "bounded rationality" in decision-making, going on to win both a Nobel Prize and a Turing Award for his work.[1] Bounded rationality is the theory that when people make decisions, their rationality is limited (bounded) by the difficulty of the decision problem, their own cognitive limitations, and the time available to make the decision.

Let's think about this in the context of today's organizations and the transformation dilemma facing executives. The natural tendency is to focus on one part of the business and then try to make sense amid an organizational environment that is highly entangled. Simon wrote that *homo economicus* (economic man) "maximizes" while *homo ad-*

ministrativus (administrative man) "satisfices," which is Simon's own term, a contraction of "satisfy" and "suffice," meaning doing what is good enough.

When enough people default to administrative man (or woman) behaviors, "good enough" becomes widespread, and performance falters. Simon thought this tendency toward satisficing resulted from a failure to understand connectedness: "Because he treats the world as rather empty and ignores the interrelatedness of all things (so stupefying to thought and action), administrative man can make decisions with relatively simple rules of thumb that do not make impossible demands upon his capacity for thought."[2]

In failing to appreciate what connectedness really means to organizations, and by defaulting to "good enough" in digital business transformation, we not only fail to bust silos, we create them. Anyone who works in the digital space knows that if someone refers to your work as a "point solution," they are not paying you a compliment; the term suggests a lack of integration, strategic alignment, or value.

The problem is that because of our bounded rationality, most transformation programs look perilously like an assortment of point solutions, or a game of digital whack-a-mole where the priorities and parochial needs of each part of the business absorb transformation budgets and managerial bandwidth without delivering the sought-after synergy or impact to the business as a whole. Orchestration paves the way for a different approach that moves past these constraints in how we've addressed transformations in the past.

For the same reasons that other disciplines such as neurology and climatology turn to computers to comprehend large, interdependent, and dynamic systems, we foresee much more application of analytics to the discipline of organizational change in the future. Indeed, we believe innovation in this area will lead to the creation of a "science of transformation" that will itself be a key basis of competitive advantage for companies that are proficient in it.

Digital technologies including AI and automation, IoT, 5G, and blockchain will profoundly impact companies in the years ahead as they adapt to the Digital Vortex. It's not inconceivable that we reach a point in the not-too-distant future where AI is used to orchestrate transformation networks of robots and other intelligent systems to deliver on the organization's guiding objectives. Already we are seeing signs of orchestration and "resource programmability" coming to the world of IT, where analytics, telemetry, cloud, and virtualization technology allow organizations to shift bandwidth or compute resources, or to establish new policies or access rules, on the fly across a vast footprint of technologies.[3]

The growth of IoT and the launch of 5G are setting the stage for the level of connectivity within organizations to skyrocket. IoT and 5G will enable organizations to obtain a real-time high-definition view of their people, data, and infrastructure, allowing organizations an unprecedented and detailed understanding of their resources and how they are working together (or not). These technologies will drive tremendous growth in data, which will allow companies to uncover hidden patterns of poor resource utilization that beget inefficiencies or hinder value creation. Better data heralds the possibility of better decision-making.

Blockchain and smart contract technology have the power to transform both intra-company and inter-company operating processes, including supply chain, legal, finance, human resources, and sales. For example, blockchain technology could be used in HR to verify employment history and training credentials, while it could transform payment processing and contract management in finance and improve traceability in a company's supply chain. An orchestrator could simply program a smart contract to execute an organizational change, transmitting money or information automatically when triggered.

As a result, the mobilization and enablement of transformation networks will become much more intelligent and automated in the years ahead. This will generate valuable intelligence to optimize organizational design, team formation, and prioritization.

All these factors will make organizations more dynamic, faster, smarter, and more agile, with a greater capacity to change. We believe these disruptive innovations will assuredly change organizations, but they will also change *how they go about changing*. These issues will shape the DBT Center's research agenda in the coming years.

EPILOGUE: ANN-CHRISTIN ANDERSEN

One year after she accepted the CDO role at oil and gas field services company TechnipFMC, Ann-Christin Andersen paused to reflect on what had been a very eventful period in her career. She had begun the journey with a small team cobbled together from various parts of the company, and a vague remit to drive the organization's digital transformation. Progress, she came to find, would occur in fits and starts. "You feel like you are going up and down, three steps forward and then two steps back," she said. "At times, you need to look behind just to see that you have covered some distance, because it feels like you are not moving."

The journey was sometimes disorienting, but the destination was equally hazy. "The main challenge when I started was that I didn't know what a positive outcome looked like," Andersen said. "In a normal project management situation, success is relatively clear. You know that if you get there on time, get something implemented, you're done. In this role, I had to explore what success looked like, which was a new challenge for me."

As a first step in her journey, Andersen conducted an internal audit of digital projects across the firm's three main business units and support functions. She also studied the external environment by commissioning an analysis of the digital activities of key competitors and customers. The analysis found there was a wide range of digital maturity within the industry. Some of TechnipFMC's competitors appeared to be very advanced, while others didn't seem to be doing much of anything. The same could be said of the company's customers.

In time, with a mix of arm-twisting and diplomacy, she had been successful in convincing key stakeholders of the need to transform. But this success was a double-edged sword. She had created a sense of urgency within the business, and with this came some lofty expectations for results. Some of these results would be realized in the short term, but other efforts would take longer to come to fruition. By mid-2018, TechnipFMC's CEO had begun to talk publicly about the company's digital agenda. Andersen's role was thrust center stage, and the pressure to deliver increased substantially.

Expectations were high, but when it came to execution, Andersen had little direct authority over the company's key decision-makers, who resided in the business units. She didn't control even a fraction of the relevant resources needed for the change. And not everyone saw the task at hand in the same way: "When you start this journey, you have tremendous expectations from the organization. People say, 'Finally, we're doing something on digital,' but everybody has different expectations of what that something is. In a company of 37,000 people, you have 37,000 opinions."

The internal audit of digital capabilities and the analysis of the company's external environment helped to crystallize areas of focus. "The customer voice around digital as well as market challenges and opportunities have helped us to prioritize the transformation agenda," she said. "It's been good for me to keep in touch with customers, even though I'm in a staff function."

In assembling her team, she started with a core group of technical experts, project managers, and communications people. Her team was small; she began with 30 reports, and one year on, her organization stood at a little over 60 people. Her "team," however, didn't consist just of her direct reports. She also partnered with the business units and support functions to appoint "digital leads" who liaised with her organization on the execution of change programs. These digital leads remained embedded in their units but had a dual reporting relationship to her and to their unit heads. This helped Andersen to thread execution cross-functionally across people, data, and infrastructure in different parts of the business.

Working with the digital leads and executive management, Andersen and her team defined three overarching goals for TechnipFMC's digital transformation: efficiency (largely consisting of lower costs), experience (to become the employer and partner of choice), and expansion (top-line growth through new and existing sources of revenue). These became known internally as the "three E's."

"If you had told me on day one that my main accomplishment would be co-creating a set of guiding objectives that defined success, I would have said you were crazy," she laughed. "That's just an obvious starting point for any change journey. But it was actually a big accomplishment for us, because it was not at all clear to me, or to anyone else. To co-create the 'three E's' strategy for our company with the business leaders and the experts as a definition of success was a really big deal. Now all our digital projects link to them, and this is quite motivating not just for our team, but for the whole company."

She worked with the digital leads to define a set of executable transformation projects that aligned to these priorities. These ranged in focus and scope. Some were relatively incremental, and thus could be addressed quickly with existing tools and methodologies. However, others were ambitious, breakthrough projects that required an orchestration-centric approach in which she would need to mobilize the right resources and enable them to work together. There was no way an individual business unit or Andersen's own organization could deliver on the aims of these companywide changes by themselves. Engagement with the business had to be foremost: "You won't get everyone, but you need to get the core people on board. You can't be a one-man band. It's definitely a team effort."

Over the course of Andersen's first year in the position, it became evident that her role as CDO wasn't just about digital—it was about organizational transformation. And, for a large, complex business like TechnipFMC, that organizational transformation demanded a new approach.

"A big challenge for us is how to position the company in the new landscape where business models are changing, and the traditional customer-supplier interface is being challenged," she explained. "If our suppliers are pushing into our scope and we are pushing into our customers' scope, we risk becoming irrelevant. Digital opens up these dilemmas faster. How will we create value? Should we take a position farther down or farther up the value chain? Traditional change management doesn't work here. We need to think and act in a more holistic, connected way."

ACKNOWLEDGMENTS

While there are four names on the front of this book, *Orchestrating Transformation* is the result of a productive collaboration among dozens of talented people. Behind the author team is a crack unit of researchers, editors, graphic artists, administrators, and project managers. Without the constant support of these amazing people, *Orchestrating Transformation* would never have been possible.

From the IMD side, a good deal of the intellectual legwork was done by a dream team of researchers including Jialu Shan, Andrew Tarling, Heidi Gautschi, Elizabeth Teracino, and Nikolaus Obwegeser. Remy Assir was, as always, an indispensable member of the team who tirelessly managed much of the behind-the-scenes logistics. Jasmine Stieger could be counted upon to provide world-class administrative support at any time of the day, any day of the week. Cedric Voucher, Marco Mancesti, and Anand Narasimhan offered important and valuable oversight of the research activities at IMD. Successive IMD Presidents, first Dominique Turpin, and then Jean-François Manzoni, provided air cover where needed, as well as financial support for many of the DBT Center's activities. Thierry Maupilé and Chris Bucheli were great sources of challenging insight in their roles as external DBT Center board members. Various interns provided helping hands, often with some pretty tedious data collection and analysis. Your sacrifices were worth it!

Thanks equally to the Digital Thought Leadership team at Cisco, including Irfan Ali, Stacey Cushman, Ali Hawksworth, and Hiten Sethi, for being our thought partners and sounding boards throughout. Thanks to Michael Adams, in particular, for his perseverance and drive in keeping this body of content moving forward, and for running point on the look and feel of the book. And special thanks are again due to Lauren Buckalew, who acted as "research orchestrator" and project manager, overseeing multiple partners' fieldwork, keeping us honest with constant stress-testing of the text, and providing her unique brand of insights on the topic of transformation.

We owe sincere thanks to the Cisco executive leadership team, particularly Chuck Robbins, Irving Tan, Kelly Kramer, and Fran Katsoudas, for their generous funding and support of the DBT Center. The company's own transformation practitioners, including Guillermo Diaz, Simon Longhurst, Mark Hill, Vivek Gupta, Chee Wai Foong, Mike Mitchell, Nina Lualdi, and Thomas Winter, along with their teams, unstintingly shared their time, observations, and lessons learned from Cisco's journey. Being exposed to the inner workings of this complex undertaking has been invaluable for the Cisco contributors to this book and for our understanding of what transformation *really* takes. As American psychologist Kurt Lewin once said, "If you want truly to understand something, try to change it."

Thanks also to former Cisco colleagues Jeff Loucks and Kevin Bandy. Your ideas in the early stages of this project played an important role in shaping its themes. Many others from Cisco have contributed in countless ways to our work, including "friends of the DBT Center" Joseph Bradley, Eran Levy, Jeff Cristee, Gordon Galzerano, Maciej Kranz, Guy Diedrich, Kathryn Howe, Jim Grubb, Tim Gruver, Anuj Jain, Christiaan Kuun, and Isabel Redondo Gomez, not to mention the dozens of Cisco teams all over the world that entrusted their customers to us for executive workshops over the past two years.

Many thanks to our editors Pete Gerardo and Bob Moriarty for their conscientiousness, incisive criticism, and steady shepherding of the work. Thanks to our design partners from Duarte, including Meredith Suarez, Jacob Reid, and Erin Casey, who helped bring our vision to life. We're grateful for the support, too, of our literary agents and media relations team, especially Ned Ward, Taylor Fenske, Rachel Auerbach, and Stephanie Heckman of Stern Strategy Group and Kenneth Gillett of Target Marketing Digital.

And thanks to our research partners, including Chad Berbert, Daniel Case, Ben Stephan, and Judd Nielsen from Cicero Group; Divya Kapoor, Vishal Gupta, and Vaibhav Agarwal of Evalueserve; John Denny-Brown, Sharla Chamberlain, and Emma Marshall from Gerson Lehrman Group; and KayCee Markle, Lindsey Smith, and Grace Floros of Lightspeed Research. The clear-eyed insights you helped us assemble over the past two years were instrumental in tackling the mind-bendingly complex question of how to execute a digital business transformation.

We are extremely lucky to be able to continually test our ideas with executives who come to IMD for professional development. We think of the DBT Center as a thought leadership kitchen, where ideas, tools, and frameworks are cooked up. Our executive workshops are like dining rooms where these offerings are shared and consumed. Sometimes participants ask for extra helpings; other times they send the fare back for further processing. Through this iterative approach, our work has been repeatedly challenged and refined. Therefore, we need to acknowledge and thank the hundreds of executives who have been on the receiving end of our thought leadership. In many cases, they were catalysts and co-creators of this work, and their wisdom is at its heart.

One of the biggest winners in the publication of *Orchestrating Transformation* has to be the global travel industry. The four geographically dispersed authors and a crew of equally dispersed collaborators have logged more than a million air miles in the process of researching, writing, and presenting the ideas in this book. We met whenever and wherever we could, including stops in Vancouver, Tokyo, Las Vegas, Toronto, Singapore, London, San Jose and, of course, Lausanne. While countless WebEx and TelePresence meetings kept things moving, being locked in a conference room in some corner of the globe for a couple of days every few months worked wonders to accelerate our thinking and iron out the trickier bits.

Constant travel for workshops, extensive writing and review sessions, and in-depth primary research all take significant chunks of time, and thus we are grateful to our friends and colleagues for putting up with our frequent time away. Of course, our families bore the brunt of our absences. On some level, books are selfish endeavors, and we owe a huge debt of gratitude to our wives, Heidi, Jenn, Karen, and Rebecca; our kids; and other family members who supported us in this effort with infinite patience and good grace. Thank you very, very much.

APPENDIX 1
Digital Disruption Diagnostic

Our Digital Disruption Diagnostic is a tool you can use to assess the threats associated with disruption for your organization, and the strategic response options that are most appropriate.

Complete the worksheet on the next page for your organization:

1. Specify the forms of value that support your current competitive position. Provide examples.

2. Go through the 15 business models (these are described in detail in Chapter 2 of *Digital Vortex)* and assess the current threat level of each on a 1–10 scale, where 10 represents the highest (severe and imminent) threat. Provide examples.

3. Think forward. Given the top business model threats you have identified, what forms of value will you need to compete in three to five years? Provide examples.

4. Identify the defensive and offensive strategies you must follow to achieve your desired future state. Provide examples.

5. Compare your thoughts with those of colleagues.

You may need to repeat the process for different lines of business.

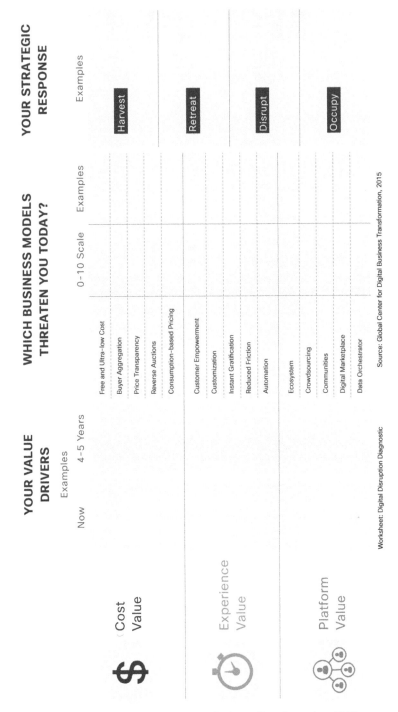

Worksheet: Digital Disruption Diagnostic

Source: Global Center for Digital Business Transformation, 2015

Source: Global Center for Digital Business Transformation, 2019

APPENDIX 2
Organizational Resources by Instrument

For each instrument of the Transformation Orchestra, this appendix details the main people, data, and infrastructure resources. Although not exhaustive, this list should be broad enough to cover most of your organization's resources.

Use this inventory as a reference when considering the organizational resources you need to meet a transformation challenge your company faces.

GO-TO-MARKET SECTION

 CHANNELS

 Channel management: partner and channel account managers, channel development managers

Partner and supplier employees: sales, marketing, supply chain employees

 Lead times, inventories

Booking and revenue forecasts and actuals, prices

Customer satisfaction

 Data center, cloud, wide area networks (WAN), extranets

Customer relationship management (CRM) / partner relationship management (PRM) applications

IoT and supply chain management infrastructure

OFFERINGS

Senior management

Employees in key departments, including R&D, product marketing, manufacturing, finance, support services, distribution

Partner employees: digital agencies, app developers

Customer and partner data

Pricing information, product performance, competitive offers

Facilities (e.g., offices, warehouse, contact centers), capital equipment (plant-floor equipment, vehicle fleets, machines)

Networks and communication infrastructure, servers, hardware, payroll management software

Cloud: public, private and hybrid

ENGAGEMENT SECTION

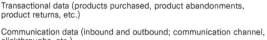
CUSTOMERS

People

Customer segments: buyers, researchers, new customers, dissatisfied customers, steady customers, loyal customers

Sales and marketing teams, customer service, customer experience

Data

Customer identity data (name, address, email, social network details, etc.)

Transactional data (products purchased, product abandonments, product returns, etc.)

Communication data (inbound and outbound; communication channel, clickthroughs, etc.)

Online activity (website visits, product views, online registrations, etc.)

Social network activity (Facebook likes, Twitter interactions, etc.)

Customer services information (complaint details, customer query details, etc.)

IT assets (e.g., databases, security and privacy protection systems, cloud platforms, network infrastructure, etc.)

Facilities (e.g., shops, branch, contact center, etc.)

PARTNERS

People

Customer segments: buyers, researchers, new customers, dissatisfied customers, steady customers, loyal customers

Sales and marketing teams, customer service, customer experience

Data

Customer identity data (name, address, email, social network details, etc.)

Transactional data (products purchased, product abandonments, product returns, etc.)

Communication data (inbound and outbound; communication channel, clickthroughs, etc.)

Online activity (website visits, product views, online registrations, etc.)

Social network activity (Facebook likes, Twitter interactions, etc.)

Customer services information (complaint details, customer query details, etc.)

Infrastructure

IT assets (e.g., databases, security and privacy protection systems, cloud platforms, network infrastructure)

Facilities (e.g., shops, branch, contact center)

 WORKFORCE

People

Employee: management, knowledge workers, transactional workers

Contingent labor

Partner and supplier employees

Data

Headcount, salaries, profile information (demographics, location, tax ID, etc.)

Performance

Building and facilities management, occupancy

Skill sets, learning, and development

Infrastructure

Collaboration and knowledge management application, social network applications, mobility

HR systems, training and learning management systems, outsourced payroll

Facilities management

Foundation infrastructure: data center, cloud, network, storage, telecommunications, mobility

Workplace resources: real estate, facilities, collaboration equipment

ORGANIZATION SECTION

 ORG STRUCTURE

People

Executive team

Middle line (managers of lower level)

Operating core (workers of lowest level, directly producing something or providing services)

Techno structure (analysts)

Support staff (helping other members of organization to perform their function)

Data

Organizational chart (departments, lines of business, hierarchy, etc.)

Span of control and scope of decision-making power at various levels

Infrastructure

Facilities (e.g., offices, shops, branch, contact center)

Foundation infrastructure: data center, cloud, network, storage, telecommunications, mobility

 INCENTIVES

People

Senior management, compensation managers, human resource managers

Data

Headcount, salaries, profile information (location, tax ID, etc.)

Performance, benchmarking data

Skill sets, learning, and development

Infrastructure

Networks and communication infrastructure, servers, hardware, payroll management software

Cloud: public, private and hybrid

CULTURE

Senior management, human resource managers, knowledge workers, transactional workers

Contract workers

Values, beliefs, principles of doing business

Products, services, publications, processes, training and development (on-boarding)

Dress code, physical layout, policies (employee benefit, whistle blower, sexual harassment)

Collaboration and knowledge management application, social network applications, mobility

HR systems, training and learning management systems

Networks and communication infrastructure, servers, hardware

Cloud: public, private and hybrid

Source: Global Center for Digital Business Transformation, 2019

APPENDIX 3
Resource Capability
Assessment Worksheet

The table on the next page provides a more complete list of the company's instruments than that found in Chapter 5. You can use this worksheet to assess organizational capabilities and determine the location of the most pressing gaps associated with a transformation challenge.

For the instruments associated with a challenge your company faces, rate the level of capability for the people, data, and infrastructure resources associated with each instrument. This will provide a high-level view of where to mobilize resources and enable their connections.

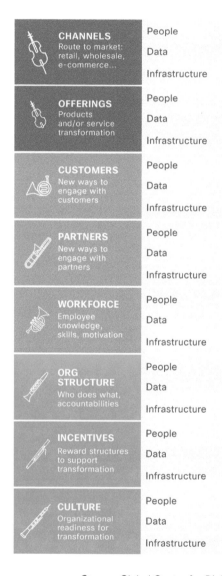

	NONEXISTENT	EMERGENT	INTERMEDIATE	ADVANCED	EXPERT
CHANNELS Route to market: retail, wholesale, e-commerce...	People Data Infrastructure				
OFFERINGS Products and/or service transformation	People Data Infrastructure				
CUSTOMERS New ways to engage with customers	People Data Infrastructure				
PARTNERS New ways to engage with partners	People Data Infrastructure				
WORKFORCE Employee knowledge, skills, motivation	People Data Infrastructure				
ORG STRUCTURE Who does what, accountabilities	People Data Infrastructure				
INCENTIVES Reward structures to support transformation	People Data Infrastructure				
CULTURE Organizational readiness for transformation	People Data Infrastructure				

Source: Global Center for Digital Business Transformation, 2019

APPENDIX 4
The Orchestrator's Cheat Sheet

GENERAL PRINCIPLES

Action: When pursuing digital business transformation, embrace the need for a connected approach to change, and operate in the Orchestration Zone, rather than relying on ill-suited change management doctrines.

Action: Ensure that the executive team consistently reinforces the direction of the transformation, along with their explicit expectation that managers and individual employees plan, invest, and execute in ways that support this direction.

Action: Ensure that the CTO works with other key leaders, particularly the CIO and the assigned transformation leads, to increase the overall level of digital business agility in the company—its foundational capacity to change. This involves creating weak connections among organizational resources that provide new or relevant information, as well as strong connections that create the trust and cohesion needed for a connected approach to change.

ESTABLISHING GUIDING OBJECTIVES

Action: Make the customer the centerpiece of your company's digital business transformation. Work backward from how you intend to create new or improved value for the end customer.

Action: Set guiding objectives that include creating value for customers, delivering and capturing that value through an appropriate business model, and the strategy needed to make it happen. Guiding objectives must be set at the line-of-business level, not for the company as a whole. The leader of a given line of business, and ideally the entire executive team, must be supportive of these guiding objectives—it's not the job of the CTO to dictate these to the business.

Action: Pursue a portfolio of strategies, with different guiding objectives for each line of business.

ARTICULATING A TRANSFORMATION AMBITION

Action: Articulate a transformation ambition—the company's holistic change goal—that is precise, realistic, inclusive, succinct, and measurable (PRISM). Encourage senior leaders to become ambassadors of the change and stress the transformation ambition in their teams' communications and planning.

ORCHESTRATION COMPETENCIES

Action: Document major digital initiatives occurring across the business to create visibility and potential synergies. The orchestrator, however, shouldn't try to "own" these projects.

Action: Create an appropriately sized internal venture fund that can accelerate cross-functional efforts and business outcomes.

Action: Engage resources that can model value impacts of transformation programs. This keeps efforts on track and creates support among stakeholders, especially senior management and the board.

MOBILIZING RESOURCES AND ENABLING CONNECTIONS

Action: Create a business architecture map of the company spanning all the instruments of the Transformation Orchestra. Map the people, data, and infrastructure that exist, as well as their relationships and the workflows between them.

Action: Determine which instruments—and the organizational resources they represent—are most relevant to the transformation challenges presented by the company's guiding objectives.

Action: Create transformation networks consisting of multiple instruments to address transformation challenges. Keep each transformation network small, agile, and focused on a highly specific transformation challenge. This makes measuring the progress and impacts of the change easier.

ORGANIZING FOR ORCHESTRATION

Action: Appoint a chief transformation officer. Hire someone who is humble, adaptable, visionary, and engaged.

Action: Make the chief transformation officer responsible for orchestrating the company's digital business transformation, mobilizing organizational resources and enabling connections among them, but create shared accountabilities and joint KPIs with the business for results. The rest of the business should focus on implementing digital capabilities and driving change in their respective areas.

Action: Invest the CTO with a high level of seniority—not as a middle manager or one of the coordinati, but as a member of the executive team that holds sway in the organization.

Action: Build a transformation office under the CTO. Keep the team small and remember it should orchestrate most of the work associated with transformation, rather than performing it.

Action: Prioritize hiring skill sets in the transformation office that reflect orchestration competencies like design thinking or business architecture. Look to an ecosystem approach to fill skills gaps, and be agile in your approach to engaging talent (i.e., develop a "talent cloud" for skills that are scarce, expensive, or just occasionally needed).

Action: Encourage the CTO to build a strong rapport with division and functional leaders; rather than competing with the business, the transformation office should be seen as a source of innovation, agility, and speed.

Action: Appoint "transformation leads" from other teams who can help thread execution across groups. Rather than creating a transformation unit that is a silo unto itself, weave an "organizational fabric" of connected execution on top of the existing org structure.

Action: Keep the transformation office focused on incubating new processes and better capabilities. Transition ongoing management of these processes and capabilities when they reach maturity to the business. The transformation office should remain engaged to adjust the outputs over time.

ENDNOTES

INTRODUCTION

1. Emma Court, "Amazon Acquisition of Online Pharmacy Startup PillPack Sends Health-Care Stocks into a Nose Dive," MarketWatch, July 1, 2018, https://www.marketwatch.com/story/amazon-acquisition-of-online-pharmacy-startup-pillpack-sends-health-care-stocks-into-a-nosedive-2018-06-28

2. PwC MoneyTree, US MoneyTree Report, PwC, 2017-2019, https://www.pwc.com/us/en/industries/technology/moneytree.html

3. See, for example, Scott Galloway, *The Four: The Hidden DNA of Amazon, Apple, Facebook and Google* (Random House, 2017)

4. Nicholas Thompson and Fred Vogelstein, "Inside the Two Years that Shook Facebook—and the World," *Wired,* February 12, 2018, https://www.wired.com/story/inside-facebook-mark-zuckerberg-2-years-of-hell/

5. Phil Rosenzweig, "The Halo Effect, and Other Managerial Delusions," McKinsey&Company, February 2007, https://www.mckinsey.com/business-functions/strategy-and-corporate-finance/our-insights/the-halo-effect-and-other-managerial-delusions

6. See Galloway.

7. Nick Tasler, "Stop Using the Excuse 'Organizational Change Is Hard,'" *Harvard Business Review,* July 19, 2017, https://hbr.org/2017/07/stop-using-the-excuse-organizational-change-is-hard

8. McKinsey Quarterly FIVE FIFTY, https://www.mckinsey.com/business-functions/organization/our-insights/five-fifty-the-t-word?cid=fivefifty-eml-alt-mkq-mck-oth-1803&hlkid=801add672349477cbd09edc6f5a9f0b4&hctky=2735189&hdpid=ccc5e256-0f2f-431b-aebb-2d5a516b2426

CHAPTER ONE

1. Ron Ashkenas, "Change Management Needs to Change," *Harvard Business Review,* April 16, 2013, https://hbr.org/2013/04/change-management-needs-to-cha

2. Laurent-Pierre Baculard, Laurent Colombani, Virginie Flam, Ouriel Lancry, and Elizabeth Spaulding, "Orchestrating a Successful Digital Transformation," Bain & Company, November 22, 2017, http://www.bain.com/publications/articles/orchestrating-a-successful-digital-transformation.aspx

3. Roger Schwarz, "Is Your Team Coordinating Too Much, or Not Enough?" *Harvard Business Review,* March 23, 2017, https://hbr.org/2017/03/is-your-team-coordinating-too-much-or-not-enough

4. John P. Kotter, *Leading Change* (Harvard Business Review Press, 2012), pg 141

5. John Muir, *My First Summer in the Sierra* (1911), pg 110

6. This phenomenon is often referred to as the "Butterfly Effect," a well-known construct from chaos theory, a branch of mathematics that studies dynamic systems. For more on how "complex adaptive systems" like those described impact organizational change, see: Roger Sweetman and Kieran Conboy, "Managing Change in Dynamic Environments: Unlocking the Power of Complex Adaptive Systems," Cutter Business Technology Journal, Vol. 30, No. 12, December 2017, pp. 12-17.

7. *How Wolves Change Rivers,* Sustainable Human, 2014, https://www.youtube.com/watch?v=ysa5OBhXz-Q

8. *How Wolves Change Rivers,* Sustainable Human, 2014

9. See Ashkenas

10. Jay R. Galbraith, "The Future of Organization Design," 2012.

11. See Galbraith

12. John P. Kotter, "8-Step Process," Kotter, https://www.kotterinc.com/8-steps-process-for-leading-change/ . Kotter's 2014 recent book, *Accelerate: Building Strategic Agility for a Faster-Moving World,* begins to address the move among organizations toward more networked organizational models: "For most companies, the hierarchy is the singular operating system at the heart of the firm. But the reality is, this system simply is not built for an environment where change has become the norm. Kotter advocates a new system—a second, more agile, network-like structure that operates in concert with the hierarchy to create what he calls a 'dual operating system'—one that allows companies to capitalize on rapid-fire strategic challenges and still make their numbers." See: https://www.kotterinc.com/book/accelerate/

13. "What Is the ADKAR Model?" Prosci, https://www.prosci.com/adkar/adkar-model

14. See Baculard, Colombani, Flam, Lancry, and Spaulding

15. Yoram (Jerry) Wind, Victor Fung, and William Fung, *The Network Challenge* (Wharton Digital Press), Chapter 17: "Network Orchestration: Creating and Managing Global Supply Chains Without Owning Them," https://faculty.wharton.upenn.edu/wp-content/uploads/2012/04/0904_Network_Orchestration_Creating_and_Managing.pdf

16. "A Hundred Years of Li & Fung: Supply Network Orchestrator for Asia and Beyond," https://www.amazon.com/Hundred-Years-Li-Fung-Orchestrator/dp/9814392197

17. "Creating the Supply Chain of the Future: Annual Report 2017," Li & Fung Limited, https://www.lifung.com/wp-content/uploads/2017/03/ar2017.pdf

18. LEGO IDEAS, 2018, https://ideas.lego.com/#all

CHAPTER TWO

1. N. Anand and Jean-Louis Barsoux, "What Everyone Gets Wrong About Change Management," *Harvard Business Review,* https://hbr.org/2017/11/what-everyone-gets-wrong-about-change-management

2. "Porter's Generic Competitive Strategies (Ways of Competing)," University of Cambridge, Management, Technology, Policy, https://www.ifm.eng.cam.ac.uk/research/dstools/porters-generic-competitive-strategies/

3. Alexander Osterwalder and Yves Pigneur, *Business Model Generation* (Wiley, 2010)

4. Avon Products, Inc., www.avonproducts.com

5. Phil Wahba, "How Ulta Outruns Bigger Retailers in the Beauty-Products Race," *Fortune*, August 2015, http://fortune.com/2015/08/19/ulta-beauty-fastest-growing/

6. Financials for Avon Products, Inc. (AVP) Amigobulls.com, August 2018, https://amigobulls.com/stocks/AVP/income-statement/annual ; 2018 revenue is based on the the 12 months ending June 30, 2018.

7. For the company operating the Avon brand in North America, New Avon LLC, the revenue erosion has been similar. See: Fortune, December 2015: "Here Are 5 Reasons Avon Fell Apart in the U.S.," http://fortune.com/2015/12/17/avon-us-decline/

8. Stuart Lauchlan, "Ding Dong, Digital Calling! Why the Avon Lady Badly Needs a Modernizing Makeover," Diginomica, February 16, 2018, https://diginomica.com/2018/02/16/ding-dong-digital-calling-avon-lady-badly-needs-modernizing-makeover/

9. Thomas Guth, "Avon Products Inc. Is Finally Adapting to the 21st Century," Seeking Alpha, August 1, 2018, https://seekingalpha.com/article/4193002-avon-products-inc-finally-adapting-21st-century?page=2

10. *Financial Times,* https://www.ft.com/content/ba296272-78a4-11e7-90c0-90a9d1bc9691

11. "The Last Kodak Moment?" *The Economist,* January 14, 2012, https://www.economist.com/business/2012/01/14/the-last-kodak-moment

12. Desmond Ng, "How Fujifilm Survived the Digital Age with an Unexpected Makeover," Channel NewsAsia, February 18, 2017, https://www.channelnewsasia.com/news/business/how-fujifilm-survived-the-digital-age-with-an-unexpected-makeove-7626418

13. "Advanced Skincare Products that Only Fujifilm Could Create," Fujifilm, August 2018, http://www.fujifilm.com/innovation/achievements/skincare/

14. See Ng

15. See Ng

16. "Disruptive Innovation Explained—How Will Your Industry Change?" Supply Chain Today, http://www.supplychaintoday.com/disruptive-innovation/

17. Cara Salpini, "Has Casper Put Traditional Mattress Sellers to Sleep?" Retail Dive, July 24, 2018, https://www.retaildive.com/news/has-casper-put-traditional-mattress-sellers-to-sleep/528405/

18. Endy, March 2018, https://www.benzinga.com/pressreleases/18/03/n11336227/endy-first-canadian-brand-to-roll-out-sponsored-3d-world-lens-through-

19. "Mattress and Mattress Component Market to Be Worth US $83.6 Billion & US $30.2 Billion, Respectively, by 2026: TMR," Cision PR Newswire, https://www.prnewswire.com/news-releases/mattress-and-mattress-component-market-to-be-worth-us-836-bn--us-302-bn-respectively-by-2026-tmr-679974073.html

20. "US Mattress Market by Product," Prescient & Strategic Intelligence, https://www.psmarketresearch.com/market-analysis/us-mattress-market

21. "Global Organic Mattress Market 2015-2019, Technavio, July 2015, https://www.technavio.com/report/global-organic-mattress-market-2015-2019?utm_source=T2&utm_campaign=Media&utm_medium=BW

22. Jeff Andrews, "Why There Are So Many Online Mattress-in-a-Box Companies," Curbed, March 28, 2018, https://www.curbed.com/2018/3/28/17164898/bed-in-a-box-online-mattress-brands-why-so-many

23. Multiple sources: "Top Online Players Continue to See Rapid Growth," Furniture Today, October 2017, http://www.furnituretoday.com/article/547212-top-online-players-continue-see-rapid-growth/; "The Future of Mattress Industry in 2018; Recap of 2017 Highlights," Honest Mattress Reviews, https://www.honestmattressreviews.com/mattress-industry-2018/; "Startups Aim to Disrupt $15B Mattress Industry," Crunchbase News, July 6, 2018, https://news.crunchbase.com/news/startups-aim-to-disrupt-15b-mattress-industry/

24. Carrie Hojinicki, "How Casper Disrupted the Mattress Industry," *Architectural Digest,* March 21, 2017, https://www.architecturaldigest.com/story/how-startup-casper-disrupted-the-mattress-industry

25. See Hojinicki

26. "Endy Snapchat 3D World Lens," Endy.com, https://ca.endy.com/pages/endy-snapchat-3d-world-lens

27. Casper blog, October 2016, http://blog.casper.com/why-is-casper-winning-so-many-awards/

28. Sarah Buhr, "Target Just Gave Casper $75 Million," TechCrunch, May 2017, https://techcrunch.com/2017/05/25/target-just-gave-casper-75-million/

29. Daphne Howland, "Casper Turns to Nordstrom in Latest Pop-Up Effort," Retail Dive, July 17, 2018, https://www.retaildive.com/news/casper-turns-to-nordstrom-in-latest-pop-up-effort/527946/

30. Daphne Howland, "Casper Aims to Put New Yorkers to Sleep for a Change," Retail Dive, July 12, 2018, https://www.retaildive.com/news/casper-aims-to-put-new-yorkers-to-sleep-for-a-change/527629/

31. Nathan Bomey, "With Mattress Firm Reeling, Serta Simmons Merges with Bed-in-a-Box Company Tuft & Needle," *USA Today,* August 21, 2018, https://www.usatoday.com/story/money/2018/08/21/serta-simmons-bedding-tuft-and-needle-mattress-firm/1050450002/

32. Jordan Valinsky, "Mattress Firm Files for Bankruptcy and Will Close up to 700 Stores," CNN Business, October 5, 2018, https://www.cnn.com/2018/10/05/business/mattress-firm-bankruptcy/index.html

33. Sleep Country Canada Holdings, Inc. Investor Relations, March 2018, "Sleep Country Canada Reports Strong Performance for Fourth Quarter of 2017," https://www.newswire.ca/news-releases/sleep-country-canada-reports-strong-performance-for-fourth-quarter-of-2017-675589013.html

34. "Sleep Country Canada Achieves 20th Consecutive Quarter odf Stong Same Store Sales Growth," Cision, August 2, 2018, https://www.newswire.ca/news-releases/sleep-country-canada-achieves-20th-consecutive-quarter-of-strong-same-store-sales-growth-689918951.html

35. "Under Attack from Endy and Casper, Sleep Country Canada Fights Back," The Globe and Mail, August 28, 2018, https://www.theglobeandmail.com/business/rob-magazine/article-disrupting-the-disruptor-can-sleep-country-canada-survive-the/

36. "Sleep Country Canada Takes on Casper," Retail Insider, May 9, 2017, https://www.retail-insider.com/retail-insider/2017/5/sleep-country-casper

37. Hollie Shaw, "Sleep Country Goes After the Mattress-in-a-Box Business Made Popular by Online Rivals," *Financial Post,* May 9, 2017, https://business.financialpost.com/news/retail-marketing/sleep-country-goes-after-the-mattress-in-a-box-business-made-popular-by-online-rivals

38. "1 Top Canadian Retailer that's Disrupting Its Disruptors!" Yahoo Finance Canada, June 2018, https://ca.finance.yahoo.com/news/1-top-canadian-retailer-disrupting-130457578.html

39. Multiple sources: Jeromy Lloyd, "Sleep Country's Slow-and-Steady Digital Approach," Strategy, May 16, 2017, http://strategyonline.ca/2017/05/16/sleep-countrys-slow-and-steady-digital-approach/ ; see also Linda Nguyen, "Sleep Country Hopes to Appeal to Tech-savvy," The Canadian Press/The Record.com, https://www.therecord.com/news-story/7310656-sleep-country-hopes-to-appeal-to-tech-savvy/

40. Craig Patterson, "Mattress-in-a-Box Retail Competition Heats Up in Canada," Retail Insider, June 3, 2018, https://www.retail-insider.com/retail-insider/2018/6/mattress-in-a-box-retail-competition-heats-up-in-canada

CHAPTER THREE

1. "Our Mission Is Powering Prosperity Around the World," Intuit, September 2018, https://www.intuit.com/company/

2. Zack Whittaker, "So Many Ideas, So Little Time? No, We'll Make Time, Says Intuit CTO," ZDNet, October 11, 2013, http://www.zdnet.com/article/so-many-ideas-so-little-time-no-well-make-time-says-intuit-cto/

3. "Introducing Salesforce for QuickBooks," Intuit, 2018, https://quickbooks.intuit.com/r/inner-circle/introducing-salesforce-for-quickbooks/

4. "Cumulative Total Addressable Market Opportunity, Intuit Investor Overview, 2016-2017," Intuit

5. See Cochrane, Shah, Murphy, Holliday

6. Ina Fried, "Microsoft to Discontinue MS Money," CNET, June 10, 2009, https://www.cnet.com/news/microsoft-to-discontinue-ms-money/

7. Vindu Goel, "Intuit Sheds Its PC Roots and Rises as a Cloud Software Company," *The New York Times,* April 10, 2016, https://www.nytimes.com/2016/04/11/technology/intuit-sheds-its-pc-roots-and-rises-as-a-cloud-software-company.html?mcubz=1 ; Larry Dignan, "Intuit CTO Stansbury on Bringing AI, Machine Learning to Businesses," ZDNet, April 3, 2017, http://www.zdnet.com/article/intuit-cto-stanbury-on-bringing-ai-machine-learning-to-businesses/ ; "Intuit Embraces Its Digital Strategy," MIT Sloan Executive Education innovation@work Blog, https://executive.mit.edu/blog/intuit-embraces-its-digital-strategy#.WcthL49OKts

8. Robert Ajemian, "Where Is the Real George Bush?" *TIME,* January 26, 1987, http://content.time.com/time/magazine/article/0,9171,963342-2,00.html

9. Cisco Investor Relations, https://investor.cisco.com/investor-relations/resources/faq/default.aspx

10. This is an example of a highly successful Occupy strategy. By the time Döpfner took the reins as CEO, disruptive competition in the form of online media and communications players had upended the market for newspapers and magazines. In Axel Springer's case, the disruption was so profound that no part

of the business was immune. Because all its properties were threatened, the company pursued an Occupy strategy across businesses. (Most often, this kind of wholesale pivot occurs in industries that are closest to the center of the Digital Vortex, where digitization and disruption are most intense.)

11. Nicola Clark, "An Old-Media Empire, Axel Springer Reboots for the Digital Age," *The New York Times,* December 20, 2015, https://www.nytimes.com/2015/12/21/business/media/an-old-media-empireaxel-springer-reboots-for-the-digital-age.html

12. Gerard Richter and Dominik Wee, "Steering IT into the Digital Manufacturing Era," McKinsey&Company, October 2016, https://www.mckinsey.com/business-functions/digital-mckinsey/our-insights/steering-it-into-the-digital-manufacturing-era

13. Michael Fitzgerald, "Inside Renault's Digital Factory," *MIT Sloan Management Review,* January 10, 2014, https://sloanreview.mit.edu/article/inside-renaults-digital-factory/

CHAPTER FOUR

1. TomTom Traffic Index, TomTom International BV, https://www.tomtom.com/en_gb/trafficindex/list?citySize=LARGE&continent=ALL&country=ALL

2. Danny Palmer, "Splicing Digital into Bayer's DNA: an Interview with CDO Jessica Federer," Computing, July 22, 2015, https://www.computing.co.uk/ctg/interview/2418752/splicing-digital-into-bayer-s-dna-an-interview-with-cdo-jessica-federer

3. Mark Granovetter, "The Strength of Weak Ties," The American Journal of Sociology, 1973

4. Granovetter, in his framework, maintains "The strength of a tie is a combination of the amount of time, the emotional intensity, the intimacy, and the reciprocal services which characterize the tie."

5. David Krackhardt, "The Strength of Strong Ties: The Importance of Philos in Organizations," 1992, in N. Nohria & R. Eccles (eds.), *Networks and Organizations: Structure, Form, and Action,* Boston: Harvard Business School Press, pp. 216–239. 1992

CHAPTER FIVE

1. Joseph Bradley, James Macaulay, Kathy O'Connell, Kevin Delaney, and Anabelle Pinto, "The Hyper-Relevant Retailer: Around the World, Insight Is Currency, Context Is King," Cisco, July 2015, https://www.cisco.com/c/dam/en/us/solutions/collateral/executive-perspectives/global-retail-wp.pdf

2. Horst W. J. Rittel and Melvin M. Webber, "Dilemmas in a General Theory of Planning," Elsevier Scientific Publishing Company, Amsterdam, December 1969 https://web.archive.org/web/20070930021510/http://www.uctc.net/mwebber/Rittel+Webber+Dilemmas+General_Theory_of_Planning.pdf

3. http://pubs.opengroup.org/architecture/togaf91-doc/arch/chap03.html

4. There is an alphabet soup of initiatives to create a standards-based structure around the "architecture" of the organization. These include The Open Group Architecture Framework (TOGAF), the Process Classification Framework (PCF) of the American Productivity and Quality Center (APQC), the Supply-chain

Operations Reference (SCOR), the Information Technology Infrastructure Library (ITIL), and others. In addition, there are a lot of meditations on where business architecture ends and enterprise architecture begins, whether the company should take a process-centric or an information-centric view of the organization, and so forth. This debate is really neither here nor there. Simply put, what is needed is a competency in mapping the nodes and connections of the company, meaning the organizational resources and their relationships; this can generically be referred to as "business architecture."

5. Haley Carroll, "How Cisco Is Rewriting the Rules on Performance Management," APQC Blog, April 6, 2016, https://www.apqc.org/blog/how-cisco-rewriting-rules-performance-management. For more on dynamic teaming at Cisco, see Guillermo Diaz Jr., "Future IT: The Who, How, What, and Why," Cisco Blogs, February 12, 2018, https://blogs.cisco.com/news/future-it-the-who-how-what-and-why

6. Kent Beck, Mike Beedle, Arie van Bennekum, Alistair Cockburn, Ward Cunningham, Martin Fowler, James Grenning, Jim Highsmith, Andrew Hunt, Ron Jeffries, Jon Kern, Brian Marick, Robert C. Martin, Steve Mellor, Ken Schwaber, Jeff Sutherland, and Dave Thomas, "Manifesto for Agile Software Development," 2001, https://agilemanifesto.org/

7. "ING Strategy Update: Accelerating Think Forward," ING, October 3, 2016, https://www.ing.com/Newsroom/All-news/Press-releases/ING-strategy-update-Accelerating-Think-Forward.htm

8. Stéphane J.G. Girod, "ING: An Agile Organization in a Disruptive Environment," Case Study, IMD, https://www.imd.org/research-knowledge/for-educators/ing-an-agile-organization-in-a-disruptive-environment/

9. Tom Schotkamp and Martin Danoesastro, "HR's Pioneering Role in Agile at ING," BCG, June 1, 2018, https://www.bcg.com/en-us/publications/2018/human-resources-pioneering-role-agile-ing.aspx

10. See Girod

CHAPTER SIX

1. Richard Feloni, "Google's Eric Schmidt Explains the 2 Most Important Traits a Job Candidate Can Have," Business Insider, June 10, 2017, http://www.businessinsider.com/google-eric-schmidt-most-important-traits-job-candidate-2017-6

2. Edward Qualtrough, "Chief Digital Officer Salary and Job Description—What's the CDO Role and How Much Does a Chief Digital Officer Get Paid?" CIO.com, January 15, 2018, https://www.cio.co.uk/cio-career/chief-digital-officer-salary-job-description-cdo-role-3627790/

3. Interview with Baron Concors, Global Chief Digital Officer, Pizza Hut, PwC, 2015, https://www.pwc.com/gx/en/advisory-services/digital-iq-survey-2015/campaign-site/baron-concors-digital-iq-interviews.pdf

4. Olivier Gorter, Richard Hudson, and Jesse Scott, "The Role of the Chief Transformation Officer," McKinsey&Company, November 2016, https://www.mckinsey.com/business-functions/rts/our-insights/the-role-of-the-chief-transformation-officer

5. IT Glossary, Gartner, 2018, https://www.gartner.com/it-glossary/bimodal

6. Charles A. O'Reilly III and Michael L. Tushman, "The Ambidextrous Organization," April 2004, https://hbr.org/2004/04/the-ambidextrous-organization

7. Clint Boulton, "Why Digital Disruption Leaves No Room for Bimodal IT," CIO.com, May 11, 2017, https://www.cio.com/article/3196037/it-industry/why-digital-disruption-leaves-little-no-room-for-bimodal-it.html

8. Joseph Bradley, Jeff Loucks, James Macaulay, Kathy O'Connell, and Erica Schroeder, "Fast IT: Accelerating Innovation in the Internet of Everything Era," Cisco, 2014, https://www.cisco.com/c/dam/assets/sol/exec_persp/futureofit/fast-it-socialpaper/pdf/Fast_IT_Full_Study_Findings_081414FINAL.pdf

9. Matthew Guarini, "Predictions 2018: CIOs Will Lead Organizations To Say Farewell to the Chief Digital Officer," Forrester, November 6, 2017, https://go.forrester.com/blogs/predictions-2018-cios-will-lead-organizations-to-say-farewell-to-the-chief-digital-officer/

CONCLUSION

1. "Guru: Herbert Simon," The Economist, March 20, 2009, https://www.economist.com/node/13350892

2. Herbert Simon, Administrative Behavior, 4th Edition, New York: Free Press, 1997, pp. 118-119.

3. "Orchestration and Automation Solutions," Cisco, 2018, https://www.cisco.com/c/en/us/solutions/service-provider/virtualization-automation.html#~stickynav=1

INDEX

ABOUT THE GLOBAL CENTER FOR DIGITAL BUSINESS TRANSFORMATION

GLOBAL CENTER FOR DIGITAL
BUSINESS TRANSFORMATION
An IMD and Cisco Initiative

The Global Center for Digital Business Transformation (DBT Center) is a joint initiative of the IMD Business School and Cisco that brings together innovation and learning for the digital era. The DBT Center is a global research hub at the forefront of digital business transformation, where executives engage to solve the challenges created by massive market transitions. The DBT Center seeks out diverse viewpoints from a wide range of organizations—startups and incumbents—to bring new ideas, best practices, and disruptive thinking into the process. The collaboration combines Cisco's technology leadership with IMD's expertise in applied research and developing global leaders, focusing on the organizational change required for digital transformation. The DBT Center is physically located on IMD's campus in Lausanne, Switzerland.

Learn more:
imd.org/dbtcenter
dbtcenter@imd.org
@DBT_Center

ABOUT IMD AND CISCO

imd.org

IMD is an independent business school, with Swiss roots and global reach, expert in developing leaders and transforming organizations to create ongoing impact.

For the last seven consecutive years, IMD has been ranked TOP 3 in executive education worldwide—and FIRST in open programs (Financial Times, 2012-2018).

cisco.com

Cisco (NASDAQ: CSCO) is a worldwide leader in IT that helps companies seize the opportunities of tomorrow by proving that amazing things can happen when you connect the previously unconnected. Cisco is headquartered in San Jose, California, and has over 70,000 employees and more than 400 offices globally.

ABOUT THE AUTHORS

Michael Wade is the Cisco chair in digital business transformation and professor of innovation and strategy at IMD, a Switzerland-based business school focusing on executive education. He is the director of the Global Center for Digital Business Transformation, an IMD and Cisco initiative. Michael has more than 100 articles and presentations to his credit in leading academic journals and conferences, and has written seven books and more than 20 case studies based on his experience working with organizations. He directs the following IMD executive programs: Leading Digital Business Transformation, Digital Execution, and Digital Transformation for Boards. He has designed several customized programs for companies such as Credit Suisse, Vodafone, Maersk, Gazprom, PSA Peugeot Citroën, and Cartier. A consortium of Swiss newspapers named him one of the country's top 10 digital thought leaders in 2016 and 2017. Professor Wade has provided consulting services, executive education, and expert evaluations to public and private sector organizations, including IBM, LVMH, Nestlé, Google, and Novartis. He obtained Honors BA, MBA, and PhD degrees from the Richard Ivey School of Business, University of Western Ontario, Canada. He has lived and worked in seven countries and currently resides with his family in Switzerland.

James Macaulay is a senior director in Cisco Operations and leads the Digital Thought Leadership team. He is a visiting scholar at the Global Center for Digital Business Transformation, an IMD and Cisco initiative. James is co-author of the recent book, *Digital Vortex: How Today's Market Leaders Can Beat Disruptive Competitors at Their Own Game.* With more than two decades of high-tech experience and an extensive body of publications, he has been a pioneer in defining digital market transitions and their implications for organizations. He is a professional researcher and works with companies around the world to design their digital-change roadmaps. Prior to Cisco, he spent seven years as an entrepreneur, running a consulting startup focused on high-tech market research and strategy. He has managed technology research portfolios in both the private and public sectors, having served as an analyst with Gartner in Silicon Valley and the Canadian Department of Foreign Affairs and International Trade in Brussels. James holds a BA (with honors) from Dalhousie University and an MA from the University of Toronto, both in political science. He currently resides in British Columbia with his wife and two children.

Andy Noronha is a director with the Cisco Office of Inclusion and Collaboration and a visiting scholar at the Global Center for Digital Business Transformation, an IMD and Cisco initiative. He is co-author of the book *Digital Vortex: How Today's Market Leaders Can Beat Disruptive Competitors at Their Own Game.* Andy develops research and insights that help guide the future of digitization for Cisco and its customers. He also works with executives from companies seeking to remain competitive in an era of digital disruption. He started his career as an analyst at Gartner, and later co-founded a market research and consulting firm serving technology vendors. Andy holds a BS in bioengineering from the University of California, Berkeley. He lives in Southern California with his wife and two children.

Joel Barbier is a director with the Cisco Operations Digital Thought Leadership team. He develops strategic insights and business value frameworks that help guide Cisco's digital transformation and investments for its customers. Joel is a visiting scholar at the Global Center for Digital Business Transformation, an IMD and Cisco initiative. He was a key contributor to the book *Digital Vortex: How Today's Market Leaders Can Beat Disruptive Competitors at Their Own Game.* Prior to joining the Digital Thought Leadership team, Joel managed the Global Research and Economics Practice of Cisco Consulting Services, where he formulated business and technology strategy for Global 1000 firms and helped them quantify value opportunities in the digital economy. Joel began his career as a mergers and acquisitions analyst for Gaz de France in Berlin during the East German industry privatization. He subsequently worked as the financial controller at L'Oréal's Gemey-Maybelline subsidiary in Paris. Joel holds an MBA in finance from the Community of European Management School, delivered by the University of Cologne, Germany; and an MS from the HEC Graduate School of Management in Paris. He currently lives in Palo Alto, California with his wife, and has four children.

CPSIA information can be obtained
at www.ICGtesting.com
Printed in the USA
LVHW020258190219
607988LV00021B/391/P